WELCOI

From dramatic beginnings on the Western Front to the current conflicts in Ukraine and the Middle East, the tank has dominated modern battlefields.

TANKS are often referred to as 'heavy metal' and these platforms are 'king' of the battlefield delivering firepower, protection, and mobility - essential battlefield effects. Since the introduction of the first British Mark 1 in World War One, the tank has been widely used in conflicts across the globe and they remain a mainstay of 21st century combat.

While Britain developed the first tank to go into battle, the Germans pioneered the heavy platform with the almost indestructible Tiger tank and the United States designed the Sherman which remained in service for decades after World War Two. The Cold War saw the development of the Chieftain by the UK, the German Leopard and later the US Abrams – all designed to counter Soviet armour. Tanks have been in action in the post war Arab-Israeli conflicts, Korea, Suez, the first Gulf war, Iraq, Afghanistan and more recently Ukraine and Gaza.

The psychological impact of the tank was used with effect in 1999 when British and US forces deployed the Challenger 2 and Abrams into Kosovo as a demonstration of intent. The 9/11 terror attacks on America and the subsequent Global War on Terror forced Western countries to re-calibrate their military doctrine. Asymmetric threats by non-state actors required a different approach. Tanks were deployed with the coalition in Afghanistan, but they proved less efficient in fighting low intensity conflicts due to their vulnerability. In the the late 2000s it appeared that the future of the tank was limited: in 1990 the UK had 1,200 main battle tanks but by 2018 this number had reduced to 227.

Putin's invasion of Ukraine saw the role of the main battle tank in the forefront of operations again. Moscow rolled more than 2,000 tanks over the border including the latest T-72 variants as Ukraine fought back with N-LAW, a 'contour hugging' anti-tank weapon which instead of hitting the tank on the flank rises up and then strikes the tank from above. Germany, the US, Britain, Sweden, and many European nations have donated tanks to Ukraine to help defend Kyiv. Meanwhile Putin's new 'super-tank' the T-14 Armata has kept a low-profile in the war, despite claims by the Kremlin that it could out-gun any Western tank.

Israel's unique Merkava tank was built after a failure to buy foreign tanks. It is one of the most advanced platforms in the world but has faced serious challenges in the asymmetric war against Hamas in Gaza.

The resurgence of tank warfare has seen new models developed across the globe with the Americans upgrading their M1A2 into a new Abrams X and the UK developing a new Challenger 3. *Modern Tank Warfare* focuses on notable tanks throughout history with a highlight on their armour, firepower. tactics and speed.

David Reynolds

MAIN COVER IMAGE: An Israeli Merkava main battle tank on operations in Gaza. JACK GUEZ/ AFP via Getty Images

BELOW: A Challenger 2 main battle tank of the Royal Scots Dragoon Guards on manoeuvres in Germany. UK MoD

CONTENTS

06

28

62

106

72

ISBN: 978 1 80282 988 4
Editor: David Reynolds
Senior editor, specials: Roger Mortimer
Email: roger.mortimer@keypublishing.com
Cover Design: Steve Donovan
Design: SJmagic DESIGN SERVICES, India
Advertising Sales Manager: Sam Clark
Email: sam.clark@keypublishing.com
Tel: 01780 755131
Advertising Production: Becky Antoniades
Email: Rebecca.antoniades@keypublishing.com

SUBSCRIPTION/MAIL ORDER
Key Publishing Ltd, PO Box 300, Stamford,
Lincs, PE9 1NA
Tel: 01780 480404
Subscriptions email: subs@keypublishing.com
Mail Order email: orders@keypublishing.com
Website: www.keypublishing.com/shop

PUBLISHING
Group CEO and Publisher: Adrian Cox

Published by
Key Publishing Ltd, PO Box 100,
Stamford, Lincs, PE9 1XQ
Tel: 01780 755131
Website: www.keypublishing.com

PRINTING
Precision Colour Printing Ltd,
Haldane, Halesfield 1, Telford,
Shropshire. TF7 4QQ

DISTRIBUTION
Seymour Distribution Ltd, 2 Poultry Avenue,
London, EC1A 9PU
Enquiries Line: 02074 294000.

THE MAIN BATTLE TANK

Since their first appearance on the battlefields of Europe in 1916, tanks have made a huge impact on almost every conflict around the globe.

A Change in Warfare

The main battle tank has changed the shape of modern land warfare. It is the single biggest change to military ground operations since the introduction of the tank in World War One. In the 21st century, tanks are used to intimidate and destroy an enemy, with examples being in the Gulf War, the brutal fighting in Chechnya, conflicts in Nagorno-Karabagh and more recently in Ukraine and Gaza. Today, tanks deliver technology and violence with the aim of using sheer firepower and mobility to win. But the initiative of an enemy with few resources should never be underestimated. In Ukraine where powerful Russian tanks rumbled towards Kyiv in February 2022, President Zelensky's

BELOW: Russia's powerful T-72 main battle tanks took part in the 2022 invasion of Ukraine. Russian Defence Ministry

troops quickly adopted the tactic of using armed drones to attack Putin's armour. The so-called first-person view (FPV) drones quickly became a challenge for Moscow's armour with a £100 drone and single operator destroying £multi-million tanks. In Gaza, a comparable 'David and Goliath' situation has emerged in which a number of Tel Aviv's revolutionary tanks have been destroyed and disabled by cheap roadside bombs, shaped charges, and the improvised unmanned aerial platforms used by Hamas' fighters. These low-level asymmetric attacks were made on the Merkavas – whose 'all round' situational awareness cameras and hi-tech defence systems were presumably not working.

Since its invention the tank has served as a symbol of political power and military strength with the most obvious examples being the Russian parades in Red Square and China's annual military displays. These fearsome monsters can strike terror into an enemy and deploy in areas where infantry troops struggle to operate. Almost every country in the world fields tanks of some description, some vintage while others such as the United States operate state-of-the-art capability with the Abrams. Germany, France, and Britain have developed and exported various »

ABOVE: The Israeli Merkava tank, one of the most advanced platforms in the world. IDF

ABOVE: The American Abrams is a digital tank that has seen operational service across the globe.
US DoD

BELOW: A Germany Leopard main battle tank in service with the Greek military.
Hellenic MND

China has a huge tank force, often paraded to intimate Taiwan, and reinforce its image of a growing superpower. However, Beijing's armour was reminded of the power of one person in 1989 when a protestor, dubbed the tank man. Stood in front of a column of Type 59 tanks a day after China had massacred hundreds of civilians in Tiananmen square.

'Heavy Metal', as tanks are often dubbed, can be used to deliver a calming influence. In 1999, during NATO's peace keeping operation in Kosovo, Challenger tanks were parked at strategic locations around the city of Pristina. Their imposing 60 tonnes sending a clear message to the Kosovo Liberation Army of power and potential effect which was highly successful. Tanks have been in global service for more than 100 years and remain a 'weapon of war' that politicians turn to in times of conflict. But use of the tank is often 'political'. Its deployment can be seen as an escalation and in southern Afghanistan British forces were prevented from using it for that exact reason – while Denmark, Canada, and the United States did put their tanks into the desert.

Tanks by Country

The Soviet Union was the successful 'second-hand tank salesman' of the 20th century. Soviet main battle tanks dominated armour in the nations of eastern Europe, Africa, and south America. Moscow mounted a policy of discounting and

models of main battle tank – while Israel has designed and built a tank that is unique to its operational requirements and not been made available to others. Manufacturers are now incorporating 'green tech' such as solar screens to charge tank systems, where appropriate and safe, while also looking at 'greener' engines. But the current trend appears to be in the development of bigger tanks that deliver more, but in smaller numbers. The British Challenger 3 is expected to top the scales at anything between 67 and 73 tonnes which may be too heavy to be ferried by landing craft and

even the British Army's current tank transporter. Soviet era armour remains in abundance across the globe, sold cheaply by Moscow in a foreign policy followed to gain influence and a political foothold in areas such as Africa and the Middle East. Countries such as Sudan and Ethiopia operate Russian platforms, operating them with little maintenance and used as a statement of their status to gain power, in civil wars. Sudan is an example where ageing Soviet tanks appeared in the first days of the civil war, but after a few weeks many had broken down due to a lack of maintenance.

donating armour across the globe for economic, military, and political reasons. After the Cold War and the decline of the Russian threat, there has been a steady decrease in investment in tanks. The UK for example had more than 1,200 MBTs in 1990 while in 2023 the British Army listed just 227 in service. Main battle tanks send a message of power and no matter how poor a country is, governments invariably view tanks as a symbol of national strength. But as the kinetic threats increase the planners have added more and more armour: the latest Abrams weighs 66 tonnes while the UK's future Challenger 3 is expected to increase by at least five to seven tonnes. Tanks have traditionally been the 'first call' into action. Their size and capability delivering the same intent as an aircraft carrier can deliver when stationed off the coast of an adversary.

Today, Afghanistan retains a small number of serviceable T-62s under Taliban control – although it is unlikely that these tanks have

seen any maintenance and therefore lack any significant capability. The list of nations operating T-55s, T-64s and T-72s is staggering, and includes Albania, Algeria, Angola, Armenia, Azerbaijan, Belarus, Burundi, Cambodia, Chad, Central African Republic, Congo, Cuba Ecuador, Eritrea, Ethiopia, Georgia, Guinea -Bissau, Iran , Iraq, Ivory Coast, Kazakhstan, North Korea, Libya, Mauritania, Mongolia, Mozambique, Peru, Romania, Rwanda, Serbia, South Sudan, Syria, Turkmenistan, Uganda, and Ukraine.

Germany runs a close second to Moscow's 'supermarket' of cheap tanks. The Leopard has not changed its spots and remains as potent today as it did when it first entered service. It has become one of the most successful main battle tanks in the world. It is in service with Austria, Chile, Canada, Denmark, Ecuador, Finland , Greece, Hungary, Indonesia, Norway, Poland, Portugal, Qatar, Spain, Slovakia, Switzerland, and Turkey.

The tank, which entered service with the German army in 1979, is currently serving with Ukrainian forces. Washington's Abrams tank is only sold to selected customers. Its protective armour and 'smart' sensors have earned it a reputation as the 'digital tank'. It started life in 1980 and gained wide respect for its performance in the 1991 Gulf War and in the 2003 invasion of Iraq. The Abrams was later used by Iraqi forces when the Pentagon equipped Baghdad's military prior to the battle to retake Mosul. It was here that insurgents captured a tank and passed it to Tehran where government scientists examined it and may well have sold data to Moscow.

Israel developed and built its own tank in 1979, the Merkava, which has seen upgrades and refurbishments to enhance capability. It has not been sold, as Tel Aviv insists the tank is too secret to export. France too pioneered its own platform while China has also established its own armour, »

ABOVE: Type 88 tanks are part of an expanding Chinese army, potentially poised for war. PLAN

the Type 99a tank. This 51-tonne main battle tank, which entered service in 2011, was China's first mass-produced, third-generation main battle tank. Combining modular composite armour and explosive reactive armour as well as a 125mm smoothbore gun with an anti-tank guided missile capability, high mobility, and represents a shift towards rapid modernisation by the PLA. Italy's Ariete tank, built in 1990s, saw service in Iraq and has the appearance of a British Challenger and US Abrams and is due to be upgraded in 2026. The UK's Challenger, developed by Britain in the late 1980s, entered service in 1991 and was sold in the Middle East. A small number were gifted to Ukraine in 2023. »

ABOVE: Korea's K2 Black Panther is an advanced main battle tank with a 120mm main gun. RoK

LEFT: The use of drones in Ukraine and Gaza has changed the shape of the fighting. UK MoD

SUCCESS AT CAMBRAI

When the tank suddenly appeared on World War One battlefields in 1916 there were no established tactics for the use of heavy armour and commanders opted to deploy the vehicles in small groups of three or four. Despite the small number of tanks available to British planners, they proved effective, and the German Army had been taken by surprise. Commanders took time to understand the tank's positives and constraints. For example, tracked vehicles were not best suited to operations in wood blocks and heavy undulating ground or open areas covered by enemy artillery.

The first successful massed tank attack came in November 1917 when the British Third Army launched a concentrated tank offensive near the town of Cambrai in northern France. The commander of the newly-formed Tank Corps, Brigadier General Hugh Elles, proposed the operation with the aim to prove the operational capability of his new weapon. The town of Cambrai is 19 miles southeast of Arras on the main road to Le Cateau. The plan for the battle was conceived in an effort to capture the St Quentin Canal which was part of the German-held Hindenburg Line that spanned 24 miles from Cambrai to Le Cateau. In great secrecy, and under the cover of darkness, more than 470 tanks, 1,000 guns, eight infantry and five cavalry divisions were massed at Cambrai. H-Hour - the time of day at which an attack was scheduled to begin – was set for 6am on November 20, 1917. The German front-line was quickly overrun, and the British tanks continued their assault deep into the German defences. It was an advance of five miles, a distance not made since the early stages of the war in a victory that was celebrated in London. However, on November 30, the Germans counterattacked, overrunning many of the hard-won British gains. On December 6, the battle ended, both sides exhausted by the ferocity of the fighting, which left more than 80,000 servicemen from both sides wounded, missing, or killed.

Cambrai was a significant battle. It showed the success of the tank and secured the future of the Tank Corps. For the first time commanders co-ordinated their battle preparation and deconflicted the actions of artillery, and infantry.

LEFT: Russia deployed the T-90M into Ukraine from the day of the invasion in February 2022.
Russian Defence Ministry

Main Battle Tank Development

The next 'global' war is likely to be in the Middle East where the conflict in Gaza risks escalation into Lebanon and the wider region. Such an escalation will undoubtedly involve main battle tanks. With ongoing upgrades and developments to nations' tanks, assessing the best capabilities of global MBTs is a challenge. Many countries do not want to reveal their secrets, especially around armour, and in the past, this has undermined several joint-ventures. The United States stands head and shoulders above other MBTs with its modern Abrams M1A2. The latest variant of the tank, the M1A2 SEP Abrams, represents the cutting edge of armoured warfare technology. Equipped with advanced features, it sets a new standard in MBT capability. At its core the 120mm smoothbore gun is capable of firing a variety of ammunition, including armour-piercing, high-explosive, and anti-tank guided missiles. This lethal firepower ensures the Abrams can effectively engage and neutralise a wide range of threats on the battlefield. The tank's state-of-the-art fire control system comprises a thermal sight, laser rangefinder, and computer system which provides the crew with unparalleled target acquisition and engagement capabilities. With precise accuracy and high-resolution imagery, the latest Abrams can effectively engage targets at extended ranges, even in challenging environmental conditions.

ABOVE: Tanks always featured in Russia's Red Square annual victory parade.
Russian Defence Ministry

LEFT: The Italian Army is seeking a new platform to replace the Ariete, seen here on exercise in Oman.
Ministero Difesa

Meanwhile, Germany's Leopard 2A7A1 is the latest upgrade of the German tank. It boasts improvements that elevate its ability on the battlefield with modular armoured protection. Additionally, the tank incorporates an active protection system (APS) that actively intercepts and neutralises incoming projectiles, bolstering its defensive capabilities.

Korea's K2 Black Panther was developed by the country's Agency for Defence Development and is manufactured by Hyundai Rotem. Meticulously designed in the 1990s, this main battle tank focuses on high-speed manoeuvrability and network-centric operations. As one of the world's most advanced MBTs, the K2 Black Panther boasts a remarkable array of features that position it as a formidable threat. Equipped with a 120mm smoothbore gun, the tank uses a wide range of ammunition, including armour-piercing, high-explosive, and anti-tank guided missiles.

Russia's T-90M main battle tank is an upgraded version of the T-90, a third-generation main battle tank that entered service with the army in 2020. It represents a significant advance over its predecessor. The T-90M retains the formidable firepower in a 125mm smoothbore ➤➤

LEFT: In 1989 a protestor stopped a column of Type 59 tanks in Tiananmen Square after hundreds had died. Jeff Widener

gun, although the tank provides little crew space inside the small turret. The tank is fitted with a combination of composite armour and explosive reactive armour (ERA) to enhance its defensive capabilities The Russian military began deploying the T-90M into Ukraine from the day of the invasion in February 2022. Subsequent losses across its tank fleet forced the Kremlin to deploy most of its T-90Ms to the battlefield.

Israel's Merkava entered service with the Israel Defence Forces (IDF) in 1979 and is currently the most advanced main battle tank in the IDF's arsenal and possibly the world. The latest upgrade, the Barak is a heavily armoured tank with a crew of four and is armed with a 120mm smoothbore gun, a 7.62mm coaxial machine gun, and a 12.7mm anti-aircraft machine gun. The tank is equipped with advanced sensors and systems, including a thermal imager, a laser rangefinder, and a navigation system. It is fitted with what many claim is the best armour in the world, an active protection system (APS) that can track and destroy incoming anti-tank missiles and rockets. These features make the tank highly resistant to enemy threats and difficult to destroy, at least on paper – although the tank has suffered numerous attacks in Gaza.

Britain's Challenger tank saw operational service in the Gulf War, with the upgraded Mark 2 deploying to Iraq in 2003. Equipped with a 120mm smoothbore gun, the Challenger 2 possesses the ability to fire various types of ammunition, including armour-piercing, high-explosive, and anti-tank guided missiles. Its advanced sensors and systems provide effective engagement of targets at long range and in diverse weather conditions. Operated by a crew of

RIGHT: A Serbian T-34 near Doboj in April 1996, during the Bosnian war. Biet Paalso

BELOW: The UK's Challenger saw action in the 1991 Gulf war and again in the invasion of Iraq in 2003. UK MoD

four, it is powered by a formidable 1,200 horsepower diesel engine. It is one of the most heavily armoured tanks in service being fitted with Chobham armour and spaced ceramic plates for exceptional protection. Furthermore, the tank features an active protection system (APS) capable of countering modern threats. While the United States, Germany, Korea, Russia, Israel, and Britain operate some of the most advanced platforms. Conflicts in Sudan, Somalia and Ethiopia have shown that ageing tanks can be deadly – even without upgrades and regular maintenance. »

BRITAIN'S MARK 1 MAIN BATTLE TANK

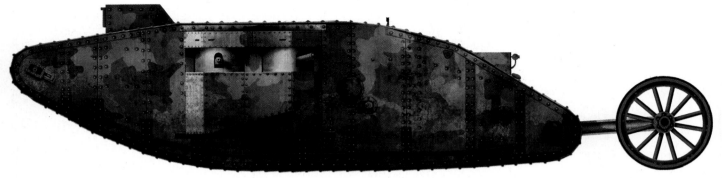

The arrival of the tank in World War One allowed British commanders to break the deadlock of trench warfare. This new weapon could roll over obstacles, strike fear into the Germans and gain ground held by the enemy. Its arrival came as commanders sought an answer to overcome the stalemate of trench warfare. The Mark 1 emerged after the urgent requirement for a strategy that delivered some sort of armoured vehicle that could break through 'no man's land' – often a distance of 300 to 500 yards - and plough through the barbed wire and obstacles that had allowed trench warfare to endure for so long.

The lozenge shaped Mark 1 tank chassis was based on a Holt farming tractor and manufactured in two variants: the 'male' armed with two six pounder guns and four machine guns, while the female variant of the Mark 1 was produced with just six machine guns. The guns were fitted in the sponsons on either side of the tank. Soldiers from the Heavy Section Machine Gun Corps manned the tanks, entering via a small door at the rear of either sponson.

The crew comprised eight men, of which two were drivers -one for the gearbox and the other for the brakes - two others controlled the gears of each track. This system needed perfect coordination, which was a challenge due to the noise inside the tank. The four others were gunners, manning the six-pounders and the machine guns. Each member of the crew wore a leather helmet, a respirator and carried a revolver. The inside of the tank was cramped and packed with spare oil for the engine, rations, and ammunition for the machine guns. It was very noisy and the small of gasoline, cordite smoke, and exhaust fumes left a terrible stench.

The tank was seen as the answer to crossing the hostile terrain known as 'no man's land'. Here both allied and German forces had fought an exhausting stand-off in which one side battled to gain 100-yards of terrain only to lose it, when the other side counterattacked. Miles of barbed-wire entanglements was set to trap advancing soldiers in the open, where machine gunners could then cut them down. Deep trenches had been dug to protect troops before the sergeant major blew the whistle – the signal for them to go over the top. To add to this bloody carnage, mortars and artillery units pounded the battlefield from the rear leaving the area peppered with bomb craters.

Tanks, with their sheer size, noise, and power inspired terror, their tracks allowed them to crawl

ABOVE: The female Mk1 tank featured two water-cooled Vickers heavy machine-guns, while the male Mk1 usually boasted cannons and machine guns. The small door made escape from the tank extremely difficult. Tank Encyclopedia

LEFT: The lozenge shaped Mark 1 tank chassis was based on a farming tractor and manufactured in two variants: the 'male' armed with two six-pounder guns and four machine guns, while the female variant of the Mark 1 was produced with just six machine guns. War Office

LEFT: The tank was seen as the answer to crossing the hostile terrain known as 'no man's land'. Here both allied and German forces had fought an exhausting standoff in an attempt to advance a few yards. War Office

MARK 1 TANK SPECIFICATIONS	
Model	Mark 1 Heavy Tank
Manufacturer	William Foster & Co Lincoln
Country	United Kingdom
Year	1916 - subsequently upgrades
Engine	Daimler - Knight 6-cylinder sleeve valve 16-litre petrol engine
Fuel	Petrol
Protection	Very limited, less than one inch thick
Top Speed	3.7mph
Range	23 miles
Crew Capacity	Eight: Commander, driver, two gearsmen and four gunners.
Length	20ft
Width	11ft
Height	9ft 10in
Armament	Male tank: Two Hotchkiss 6-pounders| Female tank: Four .303 machine guns
Weight	Male: 28 tonnes | Female: 27 tonnes.
Service Branch	Heavy Machine Gun Corps (Later Royal Tank Regiment)

up trenches and breach deep shell holes. The development of the Mark 1 tank had been based on a project overseen by what was called the War Office Landship Committee, which was inspired by Walter Wilson and William Tritton. Their plans resulted in a small agricultural engineering company in Lincoln creating what might be considered one of the most important fighting machines ever invented.

They designed and built the initial prototype tank, based on a small farming tractor at the Fosters agricultural factory in Lincoln. It had been dubbed 'Little Willy' - said to be an irreverent nickname for the German Crown Prince, Kaiser Wilhelm - it was also known as the 'Lincoln Machine'. A key conclusion from this early prototype was that a turret should not be mounted above the hull which would have made the centre of gravity too high when climbing a German trench parapet. The 'Lincoln Machine' was fundamental in providing a template for the Mark 1 tank, particularly

the turret decision, which ensured that the first significant tank was designed in a rhomboidal form – a diamond shape with no right angles. The tracks were positioned around the hull while the guns were set in the sponsons on both sides of the tank. After numerous trials and

assessments, the British Army's Mark 1 made its debut at the Battle of Flers-Courcelette, two French villages, on the northern edge of the Somme, on September 15, 1916. The Mark 1 tanks moved forward in groups of three inside dedicated lanes which were identified on maps as 'no shoot zones' to ensure artillery commanders did not accidently fire on them. A total of 32 tanks made it to the start-line ready for the advance towards the villages of Flers and Courcelette. A total of 17 had broken down and when the order came to move off at dawn, just 18 tanks were serviceable - the remainder having suffered mechanical problems.

ABOVE LEFT: Trenches of the 11th Cheshire Regiment at Ovillers-la-Boisselle, on the Somme. One sentry keeps watch while the others sleep. Ernest Brooks

LEFT: Tanks with their sheer size, noise, and power inspired terror, their tracks allowed them to crawl up trenches and breach deep shell holes. War Office

LEFT: The initial prototype tank was based on a small farming tractor and was dubbed 'Little Willy' - said to be an irreverent nickname for the German Crown Prince, Kaiser Wilhelm. War Office

TANK WARFARE

A new type of weapon required a new way of fighting and while horse cavalry tactics dictated early encounters, tactics quickly moved on.

Armoured Formations

Tank warfare has changed dramatically in the past 100 years. Today, armoured formations are fully integrated into a combined arms approach in which infantry, artillery, logistics, and aviation can communicate and operate as one force. In the formative years of armoured operations in World War One, the British had introduced 'no fire' lanes in which Mark 1 tanks advanced slowly, safe in the knowledge that friendly artillery commanders would not fire in these areas. This was the first use of a 'combined arms' operation, vital to success in tank warfare. When tanks broke down in 1916, commanders lacked the ability to inform the wider force and call for logistics support to recover the tank. Before the advent of computers tank commanders operated in 'kill boxes' which other forces avoided to prevent 'blue on blue' accidents. But as technology improved, tank commanders were able to inform their higher

headquarters as they engaged targets. During the Cold War, the Soviets adopted a policy of mass attack. They built cheap tanks and had a basic tactic – if sent into action they would storm the plains of Germany in a direct frontal attack – a move the allies referred to as 'stacks of smoke and straight up the middle'.

The US military sent M67 tanks to Vietnam, but their role was limited due to the jungle terrain, and they were mainly assigned to force protection roles – although a number were fitted with a flame-thrower to sweep jungle clearings. In Korea, China deployed T-34s and while they inflicted losses on US and UK forces, they failed to demonstrate any strategy or tactics. Instead, they mainly used their armour in a static

guard location or for escort duty. American crews were connected by radio and liaised with forward air controllers (FACs) to maintain awareness of targets assigned to US airstrikes.

In the 1991 Gulf war, American, French, and British tanks demonstrated tank warfare at its finest when they used flanking tactics to attack the Iraqi forces with speed and surprise – key elements of tank warfare. Improved communications also allowed the wider battlegroup to be constantly updated on tank dispositions. By the early 21st century, computer management systems allowed crews to visually, via a small screen, view other tanks on the battlefield and identify enemy forces, while being

BELOW: The British introduced 'no fire' lanes to protect advancing tanks during World War One.
War Office

able to digitally send updates. This was enabled through a secure cloud system, to all assets within the battlegroup. Tank warfare has in the past performed best in the open plains of Europe and the deserts of the Middle East – before the introduction of drones, which can track and attack tanks in the open. Urban warfare in towns and cities is not good tank country. Here their speed is restricted, their surprise lost, and their situational awareness limited. In Gaza, Merkava tanks are operating in a combined operation in which they can communicate with other ground units, infantry, and aviation assets while at the same time downloading live aerial camera feeds from drones. In an urban environment, enemy forces can trap and ambush tanks in areas where armour has limited manoeuvrability.

The art of tank warfare was progressed by the Germans in World War Two. Initially, the Nazis found it hard to establish close cooperation between tank units and the infantry. German commanders had spent the interwar years studying the potential role of the tank and had carried out »

ABOVE: Russian tank warfare tactics were based on mass assault of armour. US Congress Library

LEFT: The Chinese T-34 which had been deployed in the Korean conflict – but the Chinese showed little warfare strategy. PLAN

LEFT: In Vietnam the US deployed tanks but they had a limited role due to the terrain – many were used as flame throwers. US DoD

RIGHT: In World War Two the Germans initially favoured small tanks as did the Japanese who adopted this T-8=97 variant. T. Zandcee

BELOW: In the 1991 Gulf War, American, French, and British commanders employed modern tank warfare tactics. UK MoD

a series of manoeuvres designed to develop new tactics for their armoured warfare operations. These were headed by Colonel Oswald Lutz, the Reichswehr's inspector of motorised troops, and his chief of staff, Major Heinz Guderian. But with Germany still officially disarmed, these test runs involved faux tanks - trucks with cardboard tank chassis placed over them. They resolved that in order to support 'German tank warfare', the other arms - infantry and artillery, had to be mobile enough to keep up.

Infantry and artillery had to move as rapidly as the tank. In their view, slowing the tank to the pace of the infantry was a fundamental error. The German tactics therefore centred on fast, mass attacks from the flank and where possible from the rear. The Germans had opted for small fast tanks and by 1939 Hitler's armoured force was well positioned for war. Berlin saw these small tanks – the Panzerkampfwagens, which quickly became known as Panzers - as important; they were fast and in large formations could inflict heavy

losses on the enemy. But once the war was underway, the commanders quickly discovered that their tanks were outclassed in terms of firepower and armour. The Führer wanted the ultimate tank, the king of the battlefield, that could defeat any Allied tank - while remaining nearly impervious to enemy attack. And soon after war was declared the Nazis had decided their tank warfare tactics would focus on overwhelming force, they would build big tanks, and use them in force. As the war progressed the Soviets were also watching and

ABOVE: German officers trained to integrate the infantry and artillery to understand the role of the tank.
Bundesarchiv Bild

LEFT: The Panzer II, a fast reliable tank but Hitler and his commanders wanted a much bigger tank.
Bundesarchiv Bild

opted to put their tanks ahead of the infantry who would advance in vehicles behind the armour. At the battle of Kursk in 1943 the Germans began with a strong attack, but the Soviets fought back and took the initiative to win in one of the most decisive tank battles of the war.

Tank Tactics

In the 21st century, military commanders are developing new tactics and doctrine to identify new approaches to tank warfare. Improved armour and artificial intelligence-based systems which can help tank crews locate threats

are among the options being reviewed. But the priority is a tank-based system similar to the 'Iron Dome' which operates to counter and destroy Hamas and Hezbollah missile launches aimed at Israel. The system is designed to intercept and destroy short-range »

Nagorno-Karabakh enclave highlighted tank vulnerability to ATGMs. In 2016, Houthi rebels used ATGMs to destroy a Saudi M1A2 Abrams MBT in Yemen. The so-called Islamic State (ISIS) claims to have destroyed seven of Turkey's Leopard 2A4s in Syria during the Battle of al-Bab in 2017. Most recently, Hamas fighters damaged at least two Merkava tanks on October 7, 2023 when they attacked Israel. They used drones to drop a PG-7VR warhead - an anti-tank rocket with Tandem HEAT (High Explosive Anti-tank) shaped charge – damaging one tank and destroying a second. Tank warfare will embrace more technology to defend against asymmetric attacks which may see the shape of tanks changing or the vehicles adopting automatic systems such as the computer operated main gun in the T-14 Armata.

LEFT: Aspects of the Israeli Iron Dome are being reviewed for use in a smaller role on the tank. IDF

rockets and artillery shells fired from distances up 40 miles away and whose trajectory would direct them to strike Israeli populated areas. The problem is the size of Iron Dome – three mobile radar systems and a huge missile interceptor. Israeli scientists are working to develop a mini-system that can be used to provide a shield of protection to armour. Such a system is urgently needed as the modern tank operating environment is increasingly filled with threats from unmanned aerial vehicles (UAVs) and Anti-tank Guided missiles (ATGM).

Fighting between Azerbaijan and Armenia around the

LEFT: In 2023 Israeli forces did not expect Hamas' drones to be so successful against their tanks. IDG

BELOW: A restored Armenian T-72 disabled while attacking Azeri positions serves as a war memorial on the outskirts of Stepanakert. US Congress Library

ABOVE: Anti-tank Guided Missiles (ATGMs) are a growing threat in tank warfare. DPL

RIGHT: Turkish Leopard 2 main battle tank in Syria. MoD Turkey

RIGHT: The new Tigers benefitted from bespoke mechanics and a clumsy gearchange by a driver unfamiliar with the precision made gearbox could cause significant damage.
Bundesarchiv Bild

German Tank Strategy in World War Two

German armoured units pioneered tank warfare in World War Two, both in Europe and the desert of North Africa. Allied armour was no match for the Nazi's heavy main battle tanks which forced the Allies to attack Nazi armour en masse – often with a combination of artillery and tanks. In November 1942, the Western Allies aimed to stretch Hitler's resources and opened a second front in north Africa, codenamed Operation Torch. The Allies succeeded in just over a week, but losses were relatively high. In the wake of Op Torch, the Germans and Italians initiated a build-up of troops in Tunisia to fill the vacuum left by Vichy troops who had withdrawn. An airlift carried over 15,000 men and 581 tonnes of supplies into Tunis. Ships brought 176 tanks, 131 artillery pieces, 1,152 vehicles and an additional 13,000 tonnes of supplies. By the end of the month, three German divisions, including the 10th Panzer Division, and two Italian infantry divisions had arrived.

Among the armour was a small number of Tiger tanks – which the German tanks crews dubbed 'furniture vans' – because they regarded the tanks as being so big. The Tigers arrived in late November and went into action on December 1, 1942, at the Battle of Tebourba Gap. Tebourba stands on the north bank of the River Medjerda and was a strategic passageway which the Germans planned to secure. At the time it was held by the Royal Hampshire Regiment, Queen's Royal Surrey Regiment, and 132 Field Artillery Regiment – they fought hard but were overrun by Tiger and Panther tanks allowing the Germans to claim victory by December 5. The Tiger's high-velocity 88mm main gun could outshoot anything the Allies had, even armour piercing shells bounced off the Tiger's thick armour. The Tiger had terrified the Allies in North Africa who found the tank almost impossible to stop – unless attacked from the flank or the rear. **»**

Then, in January 1943 the British reported success against two Tigers at Robaa in Tunisia. A German armoured force headed by a Tiger I and with a second Tiger a short way back, as well as a number of Panzers IIIs were advancing through the Robaa Valley when they were ambushed by British gunners from No 2 Troop, A Battery, 72nd Anti-Tank Regiment, Royal Artillery. The gunners had two six pounders and were operating with the 17th/21st Lancers, who had Valentine tanks. They attacked the Germans, and the leading Tiger was disabled having been hit from the flank. Four Panzer IIIs were also put out of action and the second Tiger was also hit – although as

it was at the back of the group the Germans were able to tow the damaged tank away. The leading Tiger had caught fire and burned for several hours. At one point, while the Tiger was still intact, a Valentine of 17th/21st Lancers assigned to the 6th Armoured Division attempted to squeeze past it, but in doing so ran over an anti-tank mine. The explosion damaged the off-side track and brought it to a halt. The burning Tiger later exploded with the Germans claiming they had sent pioneer soldiers forward to set explosives to destroy it and avoid it falling into the hands of the Allies.

Prime Minister Winston Churchill was furious at the success of the Tiger. He now wanted the British

Army to capture a tank and give the country a morale boost. But he also wanted the military's scientists to inspect the tank's armour. He summoned Major Douglas Lidderdale to London and gave him the mission to 'catch a Tiger'.

Between March and April, 1943 more Tiger tanks were sent to bolster the German forces in North Africa and among them was a Tiger tank with the serial number 131. It was assigned to the 504th Heavy Tank Battalion and the tanks arrived in Tunisia by spring. In late April, the 1st British Infantry Division were involved in an assault against German positions at a feature called Gueriat el Atach in Tunisia. The 2nd Battalion Sherwood Foresters secured the high ground on April 24, 1943, after intense back-and-forth fighting against German infantry who were supported by Tigers and Panzers. The fighting was intense as Churchill tanks and field artillery gun teams engaged the Germans. At one point during the day, a Tiger climbed the hill, risking attack by British infantry armed with anti-tank weapons. The Churchills and two six-pounder gun crews fired on the Tiger. A lucky shot wedged itself in the turret mechanism so it couldn't turn - the German crew baled out and ran. There was immense debate about which shot, artillery or tank round actually crippled the Tiger, but the British Army had captured a Tiger – it was a huge prize.

King George VI and Winston Churchill both flew to see it in

Tunisia, from where it was then shipped to London and displayed on Horse Guards parade. It was eventually sent to the research centre at Chertsey in Surrey where scientists could evaluate the armour and design.

In July 1943, two heavy Nazi tank battalions (the 503rd and 505th) took part in the German offensive against Soviet forces near Kursk in southeastern Russia, The 505th Heavy Tank battalion attached on the northern flank and the 503rd on the southern side of the salient. They planned to encircle the Russians, but the operation failed, and the Germans were again put on the defensive. In the resulting withdrawal many Tigers broke-down and had to be abandoned.

An upgraded Tiger was now under review, it was to be bigger and more powerful. At 68 tonnes it was officially listed as the Königstiger – German for King or Bengal Tiger - and fitted with the long barrelled 71 calibre cannon. On entering service, the Tiger II was issued to the heavy tank battalions of the army and the Waffen SS. Six days after the Allied invasion of Europe, the Allies planned to secure the strategically import city of the Caen. The city was an important objective as it was an essential road hub, strategically astride the Orne River and Caen Canal and the Germans heavily defended it.

The British 7th Armoured Division moved to the southwest of the city confident in the knowledge that the Nazis 352nd Infantry division had retreated to Saint-Lö. As a consequence of their withdrawal a gap emerged and on June 12 American forces attacked Caumont and Saint Lö, allowing the 7th Armoured to flank the Germans and the village of Villers- Bocage. The British faced no resistance as they advanced but they were unaware

LEFT: Senior officers inspect the Tiger which was regarded as the best tank of World War Two - although the German army lacked Tigers in great numbers.
Bundesarchiv Bild

LEFT: Tiger tank 131 displayed in London as part of Churchill's morale boosting campaign.
War Office

that nearby an entire company of SS Panzers were waiting to strike. The Germans attacked with a Tiger heading the Panzer force. It was commanded by Michael Whittman, a decorated commander who mounted a lone attack to draw the attention of the British while the Panzers positioned themselves to mount a flanking attack. The lone Tiger drove into Villers Bocage attacking Cromwell and Sherman Firefly tanks but as he exited the village Whittman's Tiger was attacked by a British infantry anti-tank unit. The Tiger was disabled, and the crew forced to abandon it but in just 15 minutes Whittman and his crew had destroyed 13 tanks and 14 transport vehicles. To the east the remainder of the Tigers had moved forward attacking the British, using the

treeline as camouflage. Both sides now sent reinforcements

The Battle for Caen continued east of Villers-Bocage, the ruins of which were captured on August 4. Wittman had become a Tiger legend, but he was not to enjoy his glory for long. On August 9, 1944 in a tank battle near Caen his Tiger was blown apart by a Sherman Firefly. In the same month, three Tigers IIs were destroyed on the Eastern Front when they were ambushed by T-34s on August 12. As the fighting continued, more than 14 Tiger IIs serving with the 501st Heavy Tank battalions were destroyed or captured. The German approach of using bigger tanks was adopted in the Cold War as both the Allies and the Soviets sought bigger platforms, and in the 21st century main battle tanks continue to grow. ❯❯

LEFT: The successful German Tiger tank commander Michael Whittman.
Bundesarchiv Bild

THE TIGER TANK

In 1940, Adolf Hitler demanded an armoured platform that could do more than just break the stalemate of the trench fighting, he wanted a war winning machine that could defeat Germany's enemies and he ordered Berlin to set about designing the 'the perfect panzer' – the Tiger tank. When it eventually evolved it was a powerful vehicle that dominated the battlefield. The Tiger was heavily armoured, had a powerful main armament and would become a major threat to the Allies. It was expensive, and benefitted from precision engineering that was almost bespoke – a factor that would eventually become its downfall as the Allies produced cheap, effective tanks in high numbers.

The Treaty of Versailles agreement at the end of World War One had

stopped Germany from building tanks. However, when Hitler came to power in 1933, he directed his industrial centres to begin building an armoured force, secretly at first, and then openly from 1938

onwards. Berlin's late entry into tank manufacturing actually gave the Nazis an advantage in the new sphere of tank warfare. Instead of being forced to upgrade older tanks, as was the case with France, Great Britain,

ABOVE: German Waffen-SS tank commander Michael Wittmann's Tiger I tank is said to have destroyed 14 tanks, 15 personnel carriers, and two anti-tank guns in the space of 15 minutes before being neutralised. Tank Encyclopedia

LEFT: Hitler wanted a big powerful tank that could withstand enemy fire and delivery a war-winning capability – the Tiger tank was seen as the answer. Bundesarchiv Bild

LEFT: The Panzer IV quickly joined the ranks, and more than 7,000 variants of the design were built during World War Two. Bundesarchiv Bild

THE TIGER TANK SPECIFICATIONS

Model	TIGER 1: 1942
Manufacturer	Henschel | Ferdinand Porsche
Country	Germany
Year	1942–1945: Upgraded to Tiger 2 in 1944.
Engine	Maybach HL230 P45 V-12
Fuel	Petrol
Protection	Frontal 4in | Gun mantel 4.7in
Top Speed	28mph (45kph)
Range	68 miles (110km)
Crew Capacity	Five: commander, gunner, loader, driver, and radio operator
Length	20ft
Width	11ft
Height	9ft 10in
Armament	1 x 88mm KwK 36 L/56 | Main gun
Weight	Tiger 1: 54 tonnes | Tiger 2: 57 tonnes.
Service Branch	German Army Heavy Tank Battalions

ABOVE RIGHT: The Panzer II was armed with a 20mm autocannon, and a machine gun mounted in a rotating turret, it was a small fast tank. *Bundesarchiv Bild*

RIGHT: A German Panzer III tank, of the 13th Panzer Division, during the first days of Operation Barbarossa. *Bundesarchiv Bild*

and the Soviet Union, the Reich started afresh with new designs.

The Panzer V was introduced into service in 1942 and quickly named the Panther – after Hitler directed that the Roman numeral 'V' be deleted. This 44-tonne tank was the first of the big heavy tanks. With a V12 engine, it was fast but weak side armour, made it vulnerable to flanking fire. At the same time as the Panther entered service the German car maker, Porsche was making the final finishes to a new tank, which was to be built by Henschel and called Tiger. It was bigger and heavier than the Panther and was seen as the answer to the big tank that Hitler sought.

Henschel had been working on 'the big tank' for several years and by late 1941 the company was ready to hand over the first of the new platforms. The 54-tonne Tiger entered service in mid-1942 and the Führer was so impressed he called for the tank to

be quickly pressed into action. In August of the same year, a small number were sent to Leningrad on the Eastern Front – although Nazi commanders were disappointed when three of the four vehicles broke down. This was potentially due to the fact that the crews were not fully trained in the specifics of how to drive the 'highly-engineered' tanks. The new Tigers benefitted from bespoke mechanics: a clumsy gearchange by a driver unfamiliar with the precision made gear-box could cause significant damage. It was massively over engineered; it guzzled fuel and suffered engine and mechanical

failures with mechanics reporting 'it was not an easy tank to fix'. After a period of 'familiarisation' the crews started to appreciate how to manage the sophisticated engine and not allow it to run hot. Armed with an 88mm gun, the Tiger I tank was equipped with an armoured shield between 8 and 10cm thick and ensured its defence against frontal attacks.

Tiger crews were drawn from existing Panzer units. This meant that while they were well trained and experienced, the tactics of the Heavy Tank Battalions were unfamiliar to them and as such the crews required further training. The Tiger's impenetrable armour, powerful gun, and huge size made it a threatening sight on the battlefield and feared by the Allies. As the Germans developed their range of Panzers, these two big tanks, the Panther and Tiger, gave commanders the combat punch they had lacked. Battlefield gossip quickly elevated the status of the Tiger to 'iconic'.

Inside the tank, the crew had little room. Three men were seated in the turret: the loader to the right of the gun facing to the rear, the gunner to the left of the gun, and the commander behind him. There was also a folding seat on the right for the loader. The turret had a full circular floor and 157cm headroom.

RIGHT: The Panther was the first of the big heavy tanks introduced to the German army. *Bundesarchiv Bild*

TANKS OF THE COLD WAR

A difference of ideologies that threatened to become a shooting war. East and West tank doctrines in the spotlight.

Tension in Europe

Following the surrender of Nazi Germany in 1945, tension between Western Allies and the Soviet Union began to unravel. A period of instability emerged and by 1948 Moscow had installed left-wing governments in the countries of eastern Europe that had been liberated by Stalin's Red Army. Germany was divided, with the Soviets controlling East Germany and the Allies established in West Germany. Political relations between East and West deteriorated and evolved into years of strained dialogue. This was the start of the Cold War, and the Americans and

BELOW: Soviet and US troops face each other at Checkpoint Charlie during the Berlin crisis of 1961.
US DoD

LEFT: Soviet T-54 tanks at Checkpoint Charlie, October 27, 1961.
US DoD

British in particular feared the spread of communism. In the wake of the war ending all nations were reducing their forces and the Allies had relied on small, armoured forces – as most nations had cut military strength after the war to focus on re-construction.

In 1961 Russian T-54 and American M48 tanks came face-to-face when East Germany closed the border post in Berlin, the divided city. The Berlin Crisis began in June 1961 when Soviet Premier Nikita Khrushchev met with US President John F Kennedy at the Vienna Summit, and reissued an ultimatum in which he demanded the withdrawal of all armed forces from Berlin. A brief stand-off between American and Soviet tanks occurred at what was called Checkpoint Charlie in October, which followed a dispute over free movement of Allied personnel; the confrontation ended peacefully after Khrushchev and Kennedy agreed to withdraw the tanks and reduce tensions. Within days East ➤➤

BELOW: American tanks face East German forces during tension in the Cold War.
US DoD

German army troops and units of the Soviet army began to build the Berlin wall. Approximately 32,000 troops were employed to build the Wall, after which the Border Police became responsible for manning and improving it. As tension soared, 33 Soviet T-34 tanks drove to the Brandenburg Gate with a small number heading for the US-manned border checkpoint. This was a high-point of political tension which highlighted the need for military readiness. While the threat of nuclear war was now constant, the tank became the focus of both the Allies and the Soviets. New platforms were developed as the Cold War acted as the catalyst for an arms race.

Tank Development

Political fears that heavily armoured units of the Warsaw Pact would roll into Germany and seize Berlin sparked an arms race – which was to focus on tank capability. By the early 1950s Britain, Germany, and France were planning new tanks that could defend against the powerful Soviet designs. The Allies' main battle tanks of the 1950s were the British Centurion while the US operated the M47 Patton and the M48 series and the Sherman, while the Soviets fielded a fleet of armoured platforms headed by the T34 and T-55 which were joined by the T-64, T-72 and T-80 as the Cold War progressed.

Britain and America had upgraded their tanks with a new main gun fitted to the Centurion – NATO saw the T-55 and introduced the M41 Walker Bulldog in 1947 to replace the M24 Chaffee – although it remained and served in Korea. The T92 light tank and M551 Sheridan followed – both designed to be used by airborne forces and could be dropped by parachute. The M26 Pershing, M46 Patton and the M47 and M48 all followed before the M60, which arrived in the early 1960s. Aware of the threat from Moscow, the UK now looked at developing a new tank which was based on the old Cromwell chassis and called the Charioteer. It was a medium

tank seen as an interim platform and entered service in 1952. It was followed by the Vickers main battle tank, a 38-tonne tank which was designed to be simple, low cost and effective. The French built the AMX-13, a light tank which had entered service in 1935, and later developed the AMX-30.

The threat from the Soviet Union forced European nations and the United States to develop the tank. It was not only a weapon of war, but in the tense atmosphere of the Cold War it was a powerful political tool,

ABOVE: A Soviet T-34, a tank which was deployed to Berlin during the Cold War. Stanisław Kęszycki

BELOW: An M57 provided to the West German army by the US passes troops during wargames in Cold War Europe. DPL

LEFT: The US had maintained the M24 Chaffee which had entered service in 1944 through to the early Cold War era. This British Chaffee appeared at Tankfest 2023.
Alan Wilson

used to project military capability. While the main concern was the strategic nuclear weapon strike, tanks were seen as the tactical face of the 'stand-off' between East and West. Defence budgets in Europe had been cut as governments funded rebuilding programmes. In the east the Soviets had invested heavily and were developing variants of their tanks and producing them in large numbers. The Korean War proved that tanks still had a vital role to play - as nations hesitated to use nuclear weapons. In Korea the US deployed the M24 Chaffee to engage the North Korean T-34s, but the Chaffee had lighter armour and suffered badly. The M4 Sherman, M26 Pershing, and the M46 Patton were all sent in to action as well »

BELOW: NATO allies saw the Soviet T-55 as a major threat.
US Congress Library

ABOVE: Soviet era T-64s which formed a large part of Moscow's force during the Cold War. US DoD

RIGHT: The French designed AMX-13 enjoyed wide export sales. DPL

as British Centurion and Cromwell tanks. The Centurions of the 8th Hussars covered the retreat at the Battle of Imjin River and performed well – although these tanks needed an upgrade to their firepower and mobility.

Cold War Tanks

By the mid-1960s the French AMX-30 had entered service, and the West German government were working on a joint venture with the United States to develop a future battle tank, called the MBT-70. The arrangement later collapsed, and the Germans went ahead with a project called the Leopard. Designed by the supercar manufacturer Porsche this tank was fast, powerful, well protected and its main armament very accurate.

As the Cold War reached its height in the early 1970s the United States deployed tanks to Vietnam as it supported the government in the south to fight a communist regime backed by China and the Soviet

RIGHT: The Soviet invasion of Czechoslovakia in 1968 was the first major military action in Europe since the end of World War Two. US DoD

Union. The armoured platforms saw limited action in Vietnam compared to the heavy fighting in Korea, but even in the Vietnamese jungle the M48 Patton commanders recorded tank-on-tank duels. Washington approved a variant which saw the main gun replaced with a

flamethrower, dubbed the Zippo. It was used in thick jungle and while it was effective, it was more of a psychological weapon which the Vietcong feared.

The M551 Sheridan entered service with the US Army in 1960 and was quickly deployed to Southeast Asia. It had a steel turret and aluminium hull and was powered by a large diesel engine which gave it excellent mobility. But the vehicle proved to be very noisy and unreliable under combat conditions. The armour was thin and could be penetrated even by heavy machine gun rounds. Despite these issues, the Sheridan saw extensive action in Vietnam, being assigned to nearly all armoured cavalry squadrons in country. In 1969 the US Army reviewed the M551 and eventually, in the 1990s, replaced it with the LAV-25.

The British had been developing a new tank, the Chieftain, which entered service in 1969. The Chieftain tank was to emerge as the most heavily armed main battle tank in NATO, mounting a 120mm main gun and increased armour at the front

RIGHT: British Cromwell and Centaur tanks – commanders wanted a bigger more powerful platform. DPL

in central Europe at the time. The first four Chieftains left from the Army's Marchwood military port in Hampshire in the Autumn of 1967, bound for Antwerp and the Hussars' base at Haig Barracks near Hohne in Germany. The Royal Tank Regiment received the tank a short time later. Many of these tanks were fitted with the Stillbrew Crew Protection Package (SCPP), an add-on passive composite armour to provide increased defence from anti-tank weapons. It was named after the two men that invented it, Colonel Still and John Brewer, from the Military Vehicles and Engineering Establishment in Surrey. The tanks to which it was fitted were colloquially referred to as 'Stillbrew Chieftains'. When the Chieftain »

and sides – it was a tank that allowed the UK to set the pace in armoured development for the first time since World War One.

On August 25, 1945, Field Marshal Montgomery's 21st Army Group had been renamed the British Army of the Rhine (BAOR) and was made responsible for the occupation and administration of the British Zone in northwest Germany. By the 1960s, plans were firmly under way for the Chieftain to deploy to Germany. The 11th Hussars, a cavalry regiment, which had been formed in 1715, was the first regiment to receive the Chieftain. The regiment's role, with others, was to defend West Germany against a possible Warsaw Pact attack. The Eastern Bloc had considerable numerical superiority over Western alliance forces deployed

RIGHT: The American Sherman remained in service following World War Two and saw widespread use in Korea. US DoD

BELOW: The M24 Pershing also joined the Sherman in Korea. US DoD

SECRET SHERMAN OPERATION

Although the Sherman tank was one of the Allied mainstays through World War Two and served on well into the Cold War, one of the type's darkest days occurred in late 1943 as the US Army had begun secret D-Day rehearsals at Slapton Sands in Devon. The exercise was so secret that 3,000 local people were evacuated from the area and military police prevented anyone from gaining access for almost six months. After initial exercises, a major landing took place in April 1944, called Operation Tiger. It included nine tank landing ships, 30,000 soldiers and more than 40 tanks. However, a German U-boat had been loitering off the coast and called in more submarines to attack the manoeuvres from the rear. The US troops had started their landing when the attack began. Official reports indicate that more than 750 US soldiers died with many of the Shermans being lost.

The incident was listed as secret and never revealed until a local hotelier walking along the beach in 1970 found items from the exercise. Ken Small later discovered a Sherman tank, submerged just off the beach, and bought the rights from the US government to recover it. In 1984 he successfully recovered the Sherman, which belonged to the 70th Tank Battalion. It was cleaned and now stands at Torcross, behind the beach at Slapton Sands as a permanent memorial to all who perished. Small was honoured by the US government for his work. He died in March 2004 just a few weeks before the 60th anniversary of Exercise Tiger.

On June 6, 1944 the US and UK sent more than 200 tanks to Normandy, despite their DD amphibious fittings 43 of them sank or were crippled on the beaches. The American-built Sherman medium tank was the mainstay of the Allied armoured formations that landed in France. Its armour was thinner than that of the heaviest German tanks, but it was comparatively fast and manoeuvrable, mechanically reliable, and easy to service. The intention on D-Day was for 280 Sherman Duplex Drive tanks to launch several thousand yards from the coast, out of range of the German guns, and to arrive on beaches minutes ahead of the infantry to provide armoured support. However, sea conditions were much worse than the crews had trained in.

Despite the poor weather on D-Day over half the DDs were launched into the Channel, at distances off the Normandy Coast of between 750 yards and 3,000 yards. A third of these were lost to the sea due to the bilge pumps being unable to cope with the water coming over the screens in the heavy sea. At Utah beach, the rough sea forced the landing craft coxswains to take the DD tanks of the 70th Tank Battalion closer to the shore. Four were lost when a craft struck a mine, and a further tank was swamped. On Gold beach, the 4th/7th Dragoons unloaded their DDs under heavy fire onto the beach. The Nottingham Yeomanry (Sherwood Rangers) waded across 700 yards from the beach into deeper water that many other waterproofed tanks could not cope with. Juno beach saw the Canadians engage in fierce fighting. Whilst the DDs of the Fort Garry

Horse, a Canadian armoured regiment, waded in from the relative shallows, those of the 1st Hussars swam as planned from 5,000 yards and 21 out of their 29 DDs made it to the beach successfully. On the most easterly of the beaches, Sword, the 13th /18th Hussars supported the infantry of the 8th Infantry Brigade. Launching from 3,000 yards out, they landed 31 out of their 34 DD tanks.

The sea-state on D Day made a big impact on the landings. The wind swept across the western side of Normandy, resulting in the catastrophic losses at Omaha, yet, on Juno and Sword the swell was less, resulting in more DD tanks making it ashore. In the days that followed landing ships would disgorge their tanks almost on the beach.

LEFT: The Sherman tank memorial at Torcross at the western end of Slapton Sands in Devon. Ken Small

BELOW: A Sherman retained by a re-enactment group and paraded every year at the Normandy anniversary. DPL

competition continued. In Berlin, fears of a Soviet incursion resulted in UK commanders ordering tanks to be painted in a special camouflage of grey squares designed to disrupt the shape of the tank and make it harder to see amid the concrete architecture of the post-war city.

Design of the 55-tonne tank had started in the early 1960s as a replacement for the Centurion and Conqueror platforms which had entered service just after World War Two. The Conqueror's role had been to provide long range anti-tank support for the Centurion. The Centurion had served in Germany from 1955 with nine tanks being assigned to each regiment, but while the tank was popular it had been notoriously unreliable when it entered service. The Chieftain benefitted from a top-secret sloped glacis – the sloping piece of armour plate protecting the front part of the tank. The slope allowed engineers to increase the thickness of the armour - the Chieftain glacis armour was almost 15 inches thick, with the same on the turret. For security reasons, early prototypes had a canvas screen covering the mantlet, the area over the front of the turret, and a sheet metal box mounted over the sloping glacis plate at the front, to disguise the configuration of the vehicle.

In the 1970s The US government now focussed on a new main battle tank to replace the aging M60 Patton, and after a decade of research and development the M1 Abrams was born. Boasting new lighter composite armour, a 105mm (later 120mm) gun, and a top road speed of 45mph, the M1 was designed to match the formidable new Soviet T-80 MBT. »

LEFT: The British deployed Cromwell (pictured) and Centurion tanks to Korea. Morio Lee

LEFT: At the height of the Cold War, France introduced the AMX-30 main battle tank. The first examples were delivered to the French army in 1966. DPL

BELOW: The British Chieftain was deployed to support NATO forces in Europe. DPL

first deployed to Germany, they were heavily escorted and often covered up when being ferried to exercises on a tank transporter – all in an effort to stop the Russians filming the tank. Throughout the 1970s and 80s the Chieftain dominated NATO

wargames across Europe which often saw more than 40,000 soldiers from alliance nations deployed on major manoeuvres such as Exercise Lion Heart and Reforger. The Russians constantly tried to gain information about the Chieftain as the Cold War

THE M4 SHERMAN

The Sherman tank had remained in service during the Cold War on operations with the US military and nations across the globe. Having been the mainstay of Allied armoured operations during World War Two, from Africa and across Europe, before spearheading the invasion of Europe in June 1944. It had first seen combat at the second Battle of El Alamein in October 1942 with the British 8th Army and in the post war years it remained a crucial war machine, serving with US forces in Korea and beyond as well as being exported across the globe. Shermans had first equipped the British 9th Armoured Brigade and performed well against the smaller, lighter German and Italian tanks – although the arrival of the Tiger 1 in Tunisia in 1943 changed the dynamic.

The Sherman was renowned for its mechanical reliability and maintenance although the German Tiger was superior and capable of defeating the Sherman with its 88mm gun. A single round could punch through the Sherman's comparatively thin armour – often with devastating effect that could ignite the petrol engine and live ammunition. The Sherman was dubbed the Ronson after the cigarette lighter, soldiers with their dark humour joked: 'it lights up the first time, every time'. An investigation suggested that in many cases the crew had stored live ammunition in the open – which had ignited on impact.

Despite the Sherman being mechanically inferior to the highly engineered German Tiger, its strength was in numbers, not in face-to-face combat. Easy to

TOP: The Sherman M4A3E8 saw extensive service in Europe towards the end of World War Two and served into the Cold War. It was the tank model that featured in the 2014 movie *Fury* starring Brad Pitt. Tank Encyclopedia

ABOVE: The M4 Sherman was an American designed and developed medium tank which was built in Ohio and quickly became the work-horse of Allied forces. US Army

LEFT: Named after the American Civil War General William Tecumseh Sherman – the M4 evolved from the M3 Medium tank. US Army

manufacture and widely accessible, the Sherman tank was a marvel of engineering for its time. US companies such as the Pullman Car Company and Ford Motors were able to produce thousands of Shermans while the German Tiger tank's costly design only saw about 1,350 reach the battlefields. If a Tiger was lost, it was a pivotal loss to the German offensive, if a Sherman was destroyed, the US could quickly generate a replacement.

Faced with the destructive power of the German tanks, at the beginning of 1943 the British sought to reinforce their armoured force. So, military commanders fitted a 17-pounder gun to the Sherman which saw the crew being reduced from five to four. The turret was emptied to allow the gun to recoil, and a counterweight was added to the rear to balance the long barrel. The 17-pounder itself had a one-metre-long recoil course, and the recoil system was completely modified. The main recoil cylinders were shortened, while additional new cylinders were added to take advantage of the turret width. The gun breech was rotated 90° to allow the loader to sit on the left side.

The new tank was called the 'Firefly' and was issued to the 21st Army Group in time for Operation Overlord. In preparation for the invasion of Europe in June 1944, an amphibious adaption to the Sherman was developed to ensure the tanks could float and drive ashore. Called the 'Duplex-Drive' system, the modifications to the Sherman included the sealing of the lower hull, the addition of a propeller drive, and the Straussler flotation screen around the hull, together with an inflation system. The base of the canvas flotation screen was attached to a horizontal, mild steel, boat-shaped platform welded to the tank's hull. The screen was supported by horizontal metal hoops and by 36 vertical rubber tubes. A system of compressed air bottles and pipes inflated the rubber tubes to give the curtain rigidity. The screen could, with a well-trained crew, be erected in 15 minutes and quickly collapsed once the tank reached the shore. The flotation system was considered expendable, and it was assumed the tank crew would remove and discard it as soon as conditions allowed. However, many crew retained the equipment in case they needed to cross rivers and other waterways.

One problem presented by the Sherman was that the configuration meant the transmission gearbox was situated at the front. This made it impossible to take a drive-shaft directly from the gearbox to the propellers. The solution was to have sprocket wheels at the rear of the tank, so power was delivered to the propellers by the tank's tracks. DD tanks as they were termed could swim at up to four knots, depending on sea conditions. Both the commander and the driver could steer in the water, although with different methods. A hydraulic system under the control of the driver could swivel the propellers, while the commander could operate a large tiller.

SHERMAN TANK: MAIN BATTLE TANK SPECIFICATIONS

Model	M4 Medium Tank
Manufacturer	US Locomotive Co, Detroit Tank Arsenal, Fisher Tank Co, Ford Motors,
Country	United States of America
Year	1942 - subsequent upgrades
Engine	Chrysler | General Motors | Continental - C4 nine–cylinder
Fuel	Petrol
Protection	More than one inch at front - depending on the variant·
Top Speed	22-30mph
Range	150 miles
Crew Capacity	Five: Commander, driver, loader, driver, gunner.
Length	19ft 2in
Width	8ft 7in
Height	9ft
Armament	75mm main gun M3
Weight	30.3 tonnes
Service Branch	US Army | British Army

AMERICA'S ARSENAL OF TANKS

With a defence budget the envy of every military on the globe, the US has led the way in tank technology and development.

Tank Power

According to the Pentagon, the US currently has around 6,000 Abrams tanks in its inventory – although many are understood to be older variants and held in war stocks.

These powerful tanks have been at the cornerstone of America's forces since the early 1980s. Selected nations have been able to purchase the tank which has been used by Saudi Arabia in its war in Yemen and more recently in Ukraine, where the US gifted a number of platforms to support Kyiv's war against Russia.

America's arsenal of tanks developed over several decades as commanders sought a definitive

BELOW: The Abrams has been the cornerstone of America's forces since the early 1980s. US DoD

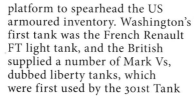

platform to spearhead the US armoured inventory. Washington's first tank was the French Renault FT light tank, and the British supplied a number of Mark Vs, dubbed liberty tanks, which were first used by the 301st Tank Battalion in France at the Battle of the Selle on October 17, 1918. The Ford-3, known as the M1918, was one of the first light tank designs by the US. It was a small, two-man, one-gun tank, carrying a Browning machine gun, and capable of a »

BELOW: America's arsenal of tanks began with its first type - the French Renault FT light tank. US DoD

LEFT: The British gave the US a number of Mark VIII tanks which they re-named 'Liberty Tank'. US DoD

maximum speed of 8mph. The US Tank Corps felt that the design did not meet their requirements and a looming contract was cancelled.

In November 1936, the US Army's cavalry branch decided to modernise, and needed a fully armoured vehicle, capable of keeping up with the cavalry and of fulfilling regular combat duties. It came up with the T7 Combat Car – which again was small and lacked a heavy weapon – but despite its 11 tonne wight had a speed of 53mph. America continued with small tanks until the development of the M3 Stuart, an 18-tonne platform, armed with a 37mm main gun. It clearly had a 'Sherman' shape about it and was perhaps the inspiration for the World War Two tank. The US then developed the M24 Chaffee and the Locust before

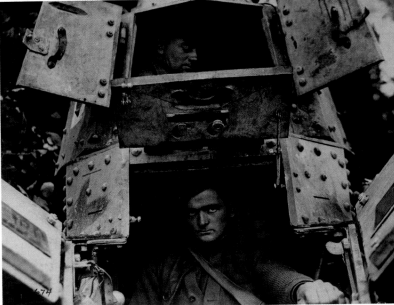

LEFT: Crew space inside the Renault was very limited with the doors opening forwards. US DoD

BELOW: America's first 'home grown' design was the T-7 combat car which was small and very fast. US DoD

POST WAR AMERICAN TANKS

M48

The M48 Patton was an American main battle tank introduced in February 1952 and was designated as the 90mm gun tank. It was designed as a replacement for the M26 Pershing as well as the Sherman and was deployed to Vietnam with the US Marines. The M48 Patton was the first US medium gun tank with a four-man crew, featuring a centreline driver's compartment and no bow machine gunner. As with nearly all new armoured vehicles, it had a wide variety of suspension systems, power packs, fenders, and other details among individual tanks. The M48 Patton-series saw widespread service with the United States and NATO until it was superseded by the M60 tank. It was widely exported. The tank's hull also developed a wide variety of experimental, utility and support vehicles such as armoured recovery vehicles and bridge layers. Some M48A5 models served into the mid-1980s with US Army National ❯❯

the Sherman M4 entered service in 1942. It was used widely by the US and the Allies across Europe and north Africa. At the end of the war

the M26 Pershing heavy tank was used in the advance into Germany and then extensively during the Korean war.

Guard units, and M48A3s were used as targets for weapons and radar testing into the mid-1990s.

The M60

In 1959 the M60 entered service and became America's principal main battle tank during the Cold War, spearheading NATO wargames in Europe and particularly Germany. This veteran tank had reached full operational capability by December 1960 and remained in service for 30 years. It was a second-generation main battle tank operated by the United States Army and having been developed from the M48 Patton it incorporated many of the Patton's characteristics in the initial design. It has occasionally been unofficially categorised as a Patton tank family member.

Chrysler Defence Plant in Newark began an initial production line for the M60 in June 1959 after the contract had been approved in April of that year. Due to the Soviet Union's tank developments in the late 1950s and delays in developing the armour and producing an upgraded turret design, the original model of the M60 series was eventually manufactured as a quick fix modification of the M48. It was equipped with a 105mm, M68 main gun with a bore evacuator – which extracts lingering gases from fired ammunition in the crew space - positioned towards the centre of the tube. A total of 57

rounds were held in the M48 adopted turret and a further nine rounds were concealed below the loader on the left side of the turret tray.

The M60 was designed to use revolutionary composite armour which comprised layers of different material such as metals, plastics, ceramics, or air. This revolutionary armour could withstand bigger blasts than traditional all-steel rolled homogeneous armour. However, despite being able to withstand initial impacts better than steel, it was found that the composite panels quickly deteriorated, and the regular refurbishment required added to costs, so designers opted to go with an all-steel design, making

the M60 the last American tank to have all-steel armour. When hull manufacture came to a halt in 1983, more than 5,000 older vehicles were upgraded which included increasing the turret armour thickness and changing the flammable hydraulic fluid in the turret for a non-flammable alternative.

The tank proved itself during the Gulf War with US Marine tank crews reporting that the armour upgrade allowed it to head the advance towards Kuwait International Airport, destroying hundreds of Iraqi T-55s and T-62s, as well as several of the then-dominant Soviet-designed T-72s and a number of armoured personnel carriers and vehicles. »

ABOVE: The M60 was widely exported with Jordan purchasing several hundred.
US DoD

LEFT: In the 1991 Gulf War the US Marines deployed the M60.
US DoD

ABOVE: In several incidents during the Gulf War USMC M60s engaged and destroyed Iraqi T-72s. US DoD

RIGHT: The M551 was an airborne tank which entered service in 1960 and was used by the 3rd Battalion (Airborne) 73rd Armored Cavalry Regiment during the 1991 Gulf War. US DoD

The M60 tank-on-tank combat in the Gulf War was the largest in US Marine Corps history. The M60A3 tanks used by the USMC were later replaced by the Abrams tanks and formally retired from US military service. After Operation Desert Storm, the US stopped using the M60 in front-line combat and those in service with the National Guard were de-commissioned in 1997.

The M551

In the early 1960s the US Army needed a light tank capable of supporting airborne operations and built the M551 Sheridan, an airborne deployable reconnaissance tank, which was used by the 3rd battalion (Airborne) 73rd Armored Cavalry Regiment in the 1991 Gulf War. It was deployed with a thermal sight upgrade and was assigned to a flank protection role which saw crews involved in tank-on-tank combat.

The Sheridan was adopted by the US Army in 1967 and, following the American tradition of naming armour after notable army generals, was named after General Philip Sheridan.

Weighing approximately sixteen tons, the M551 Sheridan's hull was constructed from aluminium alloy, while the turret was made of steel. The Sheridan was 22ft long and just over 13ft wide. Powered by a General Motors 6V53T, six cylinder 300-horsepower supercharged diesel engine, the Sheridan could reach road speeds of nearly 45mph. It had a cruising range of 373 miles and was amphibious, capable of swimming across water obstacles at a speed of 4mph. It could also be air dropped to provide fire support to airborne units.

The key element of the new tank was the untried XM81 gun-missile launcher system capable of firing both 152mm cannon rounds and the Shillelagh missile. Unlike previous tank gun rounds that used conventional brass shell casings, the XM81 fired rounds with combustible cartridge cases. Early variants of the type were deployed to Vietnam, which highlighted the platform's flaws, particularly its poor survivability and dependability. It was later sent to South Korea and also assigned to US battalions based in Europe.

Despite the fact that there was no true substitute at the time, the US Army began to phase out the Sheridan in 1978 – although the 82nd Airborne Division was allowed to retain them until 1996. During the US invasion of Panama in 1989 - Operation Just Cause - a total of 14 Sheridan tanks were deployed with C Company, 3/73rd of the 82nd Airborne, marking the Sheridan's sole combat air drop during its years of service. And, in 1990, during Operation Desert Shield, the build of coalition forces in the Gulf, Sheridan tanks were airlanded in Saudi Arabia during the early stages of the mission, before heavier armour arrived via ship. The US Army also hurriedly delivered 60 M551A1 TTS variants with the thermal sight modification ready for operations. During Operation Desert Storm, the 3/73 Cavalry were tasked to protect the main force in a screening role and found themselves engaged in combat with the Iraqis. This was the only time Shillelagh missiles were fired in anger. Their light armour and advanced age restricted them to a reconnaissance mission during Desert Shield.

RIGHT: The Abrams remains America's main battle tank, ready for operations anywhere in the world. US DoD

through a secret radio system, known as Sincgars, to maintain what the military term 'secure' communications – which cannot be intercepted.

In 2003, US and Coalition forces were back in the Middle East for what remains the most controversial conflict since World War Two. Unlike the common consent reached in the Gulf War of 1991 (Operation Desert Storm), the 2003 war saw no widespread military coalition to remove Saddam from power. Some European leaders expressed conditional support for the war, but Germany and France voiced their opposition over the conditions for going to war and declined to send military forces to participate in the invasion. Many nations in the Gulf region saw it as a new brand of anti-Arab and anti-Islamic imperialism. Arab leaders objected to the occupation of a fellow Arab country by foreign troops and by late 2002 Washington was unclear as to exactly what level of armour other Coalition nations would commit to the conflict. The United States prepared to deploy a substantial armoured force. The upgraded Abrams M1A2 main battle tank was sent into action alongside the M1A1s. This time, instead of ejecting Iraqi forces from Kuwait the Abrams would drive across the desert to Baghdad, eject Saddam and his forces, and seize the capital.

On the morning of April 3, 2003, US forces advanced on Baghdad International Airport which turned out to be the best defended Iraqi position of the entire war. After several hours of combat, the First Brigade, Third Infantry Division succeeded in taking control of the airport, which would become the hub of American logistics in Iraq

ABOVE: Abrams in Iraq fitted with the enhanced explosive reactive armoured protection called TUSK. US Army

LEFT: Abrams crews spend up to six months of the year training both in the United States and overseas. US Army

for the next seven years. On April 4, US troops were subjected to a fierce counterattack by Iraqi troops. The First Brigade's Tactical Operations Centre (TOC) began receiving small arms and mortar fire and under the cover of darkness, a number of Iraqi T-72 tanks had managed to get

within 600 yards of their position. The Iraqi T-72s opened fire hitting a Fuchs chemical vehicle and a Bradley. US forces quickly responded, and a Javelin team destroyed two of the tanks while an Abrams was called in to mount a counterattack which silenced »

BELOW: Abrams tanks in formation race across the desert during Operation Desert Storm in 1990. US Army

the enemy tanks. On the same day the 2nd Tank Battalion of the US Marine Corps had a challenging fight with the Al Nida Division of the Republican Guards and a large contingent of foreign Islamist fighters on the outskirts of Baghdad in which an Abrams was lost. Two Abrams of the 5th Regimental Combat Team were destroyed while engaged with the Fedayeen and Al Nida Republican Guards, who fired anti-aircraft guns at the USMC tanks in the ground role.

Also, on April 4 the US Army's 3rd Infantry Division (3ID) was forced to abandon one of its tanks due to a rocket attack to the rear of the Abrams that penetrated a fuel cell and set the engine on fire. The crew was unharmed. Later, the US Air Force bombed the tank to destroy it in place. On the morning of April 7, 2003, two battalions of M1A1 Abrams tanks and Bradley

Fighting Vehicles from the 3rd Infantry Division's 2nd Brigade had staged what was called the second 'Thunder Run', advancing into the exclusive 'regime zone' on the west bank of the Tigris River. A group of M1A1s engaged seven T-72s in a point-blank skirmish at a range of less than 100 yards near the town of Mahmudiyah, about 18 miles south of Baghdad – there were no US losses. The 2nd Brigade faced

sporadic attacks before securing Saddam's palaces. The 'Thunder Runs' had been a bold move and had assured the advance into Baghdad and the quick seizure of key areas within the city.

As they advanced, the 2nd Brigade's Abrams had to secure Highway 8 from the south which would become the vital supply line that would sustain the assault force. Key to that challenge was occupying three intersections — dubbed by army planners in a lighter moment as Objectives 'Moe', 'Larry' and 'Curly', stars of the American comedy the *Three Stooges*. Intense fighting took place at the three locations. Each objective was a cloverleaf – an American term for

LEFT: As planners look to the future, a concept called the Abrams X was unveiled at a 2023 defence show in the US. US Army

an interstate road where east–west roads intersected with the main north–south route. Successfully holding these highway interchanges was essential to keep Highway 8 open and allowing US forces to remain in the city centre following the second Thunder Run. Objective Moe was at the junction of Highway 8 and the Qadisiyah expressway, Larry at Qatar Al-Nada street leading to the Al Jadriyah bridge, and Curly at the Dora expressway. At Objective Curly, an 18-hour battle by the 3–15 Infantry resulted in them nearly running out of fuel and ammunition and they were almost overrun when reinforcements broke through and were able to resupply them.

LEFT: The driving controls of the Abrams, the driving and steering yoke differs from many other main battle tanks that use tiller sticks. US Army

BELOW: In 2023 the United States donated dozens of Abrams tanks to Ukraine to support President Zelensky's fight against Russia. US Army »

ABRAMS M1A1

form-fitting bucket seat. M1 crew members say that this is far and away the most comfortable position in the tank. The driver steers the tank using a motorcycle-style handlebar and accelerates by twisting a handle grip throttle on the right-hand side. The tank has a brake pedal on the floor, just like a car and was the first tank of its kind to be fitted with Chobham armour, which had been developed by Britain's Military Vehicles and Engineering Establishment. Although the construction details of the Chobham armour remain secret, it has been described as being composed of ceramic tiles encased within a metal framework and bonded to a backing plate of several elastic layers. Owing to the extreme hardness of the ceramics used, they offer superior resistance against shaped charges such as high explosive anti-tank (HEAT) rounds – due to the fact that they shatter the kinetic energy of the incoming missile.

The Abrams first saw combat in the 1991 Gulf War, during

M1 ABRAMS SPECIFICATION

Model	M1A1 later upgraded M1A2
Manufacturer	General Dynamics Land Systems
Country	United States
Year	1992 onwards
Engine	1,500hp gas turbine engine
Fuel	Diesel
Protection	Chobham armour and uranium plates
Top Speed	42mph on road (67kph)
Range	265 miles (426km)
Crew Capacity	Four
Length	32ft
Width	12ft
Height	8ft
Armament	120mm M256 smoothbore
Secondary Armament	One coaxial 7.62mm, one top turret 7.62mm machine gun and one 12.7mm anti-aircraft machine gun
Weight	67 tonnes
Service Branch	US Army, USMC

The Abrams is designed for a four-person crew. The driver sits in the front section of the hull, directly under the main gun in a seat that is almost fully reclined. In order to fit in the very confined space, he has to lean way back to access the

Operation Desert Storm. The US Army deployed a total of 1,956 Abrams M1A1s to Saudi Arabia to participate in the liberation of Kuwait. Among them was the Improved Performance M1 (IPM1) which was a stop-gap vehicle, featuring numerous upgrades; a new turret, sometimes referred to as the 'long turret', which offered greater protection and a rear turret bustle rack for more stowage space for crew equipment. There were also some improvements to the suspension and powerpack to accommodate the heavier turret and the rear side skirts were improved.

The M1 had initially been fitted with a 105mm main gun while later variants featured a licence-produced Rheinmetall 120mm main gun. The Abrams was superior to Iraq's Soviet era tanks, which included the T-54 and T-55 as well as the T-62 and T-72. The Iraqi tanks lacked modern technology such as night-vision and, in many cases, no clear doctrine as to how to operate their armour on the battlefield. While no Abrams were destroyed by Iraqi forces, three were abandoned during an attack on the Talil airfield, south of Nasiriyah. One of the Abrams was hit and disabled and two others were embedded in heavy mud. All three tanks were 'denied' (destroyed) by a US airstrike to avoid any trophy claim by the Iraqis. A total of 23 M1A1s were damaged or destroyed during the war. Of the nine Abrams tanks actually destroyed, seven were as a result of accidental friendly fire and two intentionally destroyed to prevent capture by the Iraqi army. No M1s were lost to enemy tank fire.

Some others took minor combat damage, with little effect on their operational readiness.

Since its entry into service, the M1 Abrams tank has been the spearhead of US Army ground

forces, providing mobility, protection, and precision firepower on the battlefield. Dubbed by workers at the Lima Tank Plant as the 'beast of Ohio' it is a heavy tank packed with technology. After the conflict a US State Department study reported that several M1A1 crews reported receiving direct frontal hits from Iraqi T-72s in which they sustained minimal damage. Several years later the upgraded M1A2 spearheaded the race to Baghdad when US armoured forces motored across the desert in what was described as a 'Thunder Run' to oust Saddam Hussein and seize the capital during Operation Iraqi Freedom.

The Abrams' powerful gas turbine engine can propel the tank through almost any terrain, from snow, heavy mud, or fine desert sand. With a crew of four, the Abrams has thick armour, a 120mm main gun with an armour piercing capability. It benefits from advanced targeting systems, thick tracked wheels, and a 1,500-horsepower powerplant capable of delivering a top speed of about 42mph.

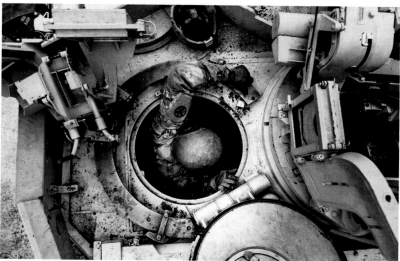

BRITISH TANKS

With a heritage that stretches all the way back to the first operational tank, the UK remains at the cutting edge of armour development.

ABOVE: The Crusader tank entered service in 1941, more than 5,000 were produced.
War Office

Tank Development

Britain pioneered the development of the tank and has remained committed to armoured warfare, deploying tanks across Europe and North Africa, the Middle East and more recently in eastern Europe. World War One established the importance of the tank and following that conflict, many nations sought an armoured capability, but only a few had the industrial resources to design and build them. During and after the war, Britain and France were the intellectual pioneers in tank design, with other countries generally following and adopting their designs. This early advantage was gradually lost during the course of the 1930s as the Soviet Union invested heavily in the tank as did Germany. With the

RIGHT: British troops re-capture a Matilda tank from the Germans in the North African desert.
War Office

outbreak of World War Two the UK and then America focused on the mass production of wartime tanks to overcome the Germans but when the war ended it was clear that Moscow had ramped up its production to outnumber their wartime allies forces.

When Germany was partitioned sparking the Cold War, the Western allies quickly sought solutions to build new platforms and upgrade existing tanks. World War Two had seen the British develop a vast fleet of armour which included the Cruiser tank, the Matilda, the Valentine, Churchill, Cromwell, and Comet. Additionally, Britain had received »

ABOVE: The Matilda entered service in 1939 with the British Army and remained in operation after World War Two.
War Office

LEFT: A British Valentine tank in North Africa – the tanks had a reputation for being unreliable.
War Office

LEFT: A Valentine tank fitted with Duplex Drive amphibious equipment for the D-Day landings. War Office

large numbers of Sherman tanks from the United States and as D-Day approached many were converted to carry a bigger gun and re-designated as Sherman Fireflys. In the post war years, the Centurion and Conqueror entered service, but as the threat from the Red Army increased, military commanders wanted a bigger, more powerful tank with a larger gun to challenge the capability of the Soviet armour.

Studies had been ongoing since the end of the war, but most nations were reducing defence expenditure and investing in post-war society. However, military planners wanted to build on the success of the Centurion which had been introduced just 12 months after the end of the conflict . It was a 50-tonne platform with a 105mm main gun and a crew of four. It had been in development since 1943, when the Directorate of Tank Design was asked to produce a new design for a heavy cruiser tank which was

BELOW: Churchill tanks of the 9th Royal Tank Regiment during an exercise on Salisbury Plain in the UK in January 1942. War Office

listed as project A41, and which eventually became the Centurion . The Centurion had better armour protection and survivability than the American M48, whose transmission fluid was prone to catch on fire when the vehicle was hit. But in the early 1960s, Britain needed a new tank, and plans were underway for the Chieftain – in the meantime the Centurion remained the UK's main tank.

NATO planners were becoming increasingly concerned at the numbers of T-34 tanks in service with the Warsaw Pact countries and by early 1952, the Western alliance was gently pressing members to base armour in Germany. Britain had established the British Army on the Rhine (BAOR), the French deployed the AMX-13 to their sector and the Americans supported the supply of Centurions to Denmark and the Netherlands under the Mutual Defence Assistance Programme. **»**

ABOVE: Comet tanks of the 2nd Fife and Forfar Yeomanry serving with the 11th Armoured Division on the outskirts of Germany in April 1945. War Office

LEFT: A Cromwell of the King's Royal Hussars advances through Uedem in Germany in early 1945. War Office

ABOVE LEFT: A British Sherman, secured from the US under Lend-Lease, in North Africa. War Office

ABOVE RIGHT: Sherman 'Duplex Drive' tanks near Ouistreham shortly after the landings in June 1944. AFPU

RIGHT: A British Sherman Firefly pictured in Germany in 1945. War Office

Centurion Operations

In November 1950, the British Army's 8th King's Royal Irish Hussars equipped with three squadrons – a total of 64 tanks – landed at Pusan in Korea where they fought in sub-zero temperatures and were joined by more Centurions from the 5th Royal Inniskilling Dragoon Guards and the Royal Tank Regiment, tasked to repel the Chinese. A senior commander stated: "In their Centurions, the 8th Hussars have evolved a new type of tank warfare. They taught us that anywhere a tank can go, is tank country - even the tops of mountains." However, the lack of pintle-mounted machine guns on the turret meant that the Centurion was only able to fire in one direction and so was vulnerable to infantry attacks.

Centurions were in action again in 1956 when the UK and France landed at Suez. In planning for operations in

RIGHT: Prime Minister Winston Churchill inspecting a Cromwell tank. War Office

RIGHT: British Centurion tanks were landed at Suez in 1956. MoD

Egypt the British ground commander General Sir Hugh Stockwell believed that armoured operations centred on the Centurion would be the key to victory. Centurions of the 6th Royal Tank Regiment were landed and linked up with French and British paratroopers. The Centurions later supported Royal Marines in clearing Port Said. The Centurion tank had earned a good reputation and had been procured by Israel, South Africa, Sweden, Pakistan, and Australia. In 1968 the Royal Australian Armoured Corps deployed their Centurions to south Vietnam. Pakistan used its Centurions in operations

BELOW: The British Centurion engineer variant was used in Northern Ireland to remove barricades. MoD

against Indian forces in the battle of Chawinda.

In Northern Ireland, the Armoured Vehicle Royal Engineers (AVREs) variant of the Centurion was deployed in 1972 to support Operation Motorman. Armed with a 165mm main gun, which was not used, the tanks' bulldozer blades were used to destroy barricades set up in Northern Ireland. And during Operation Desert Storm in 1991, Centurion AVREs were deployed with 32 Armoured Engineer Regiment. Three were lost in training in two separate incidents involving vehicle fires and detonation of munitions. One AVRE was destroyed on February 5, 1991 and two were destroyed in a second incident the next day. Four minor injuries were sustained. No AVRES saw action during the operation.

Israeli Venture

The early development of the Chieftain had included a joint-venture with Israel. The project started in the 1960s when Britain sold more than 200 Centurions to Israel with plans to also sell the new Chieftain to the Tel Aviv government too. And a four-year study which included the delivery of two prototypes was part of a deal that was to see the new tank built in Israel. However, following the Six Day War between Israel and Arab states in 1967, the UK government expressed concern about peace in the Middle East and the effect the development partnership would have on the UK's relationship with Arab

countries. The then foreign secretary, Michael Stewart wrote to the Israeli ambassador in London, Aharon Remez and said: "We are concerned about the impact of major deliveries of arms of this kind on the prospects for peace in the Middle East." And, in the autumn of 1969, the British government decided not to go ahead with the sale. The Israeli Prime Minister Mrs Golda Meir told the Knesset on December 15, that Britain 'was favouring the Arab states." And, in 1973, the Conservative government of Edward Heath imposed an arms embargo on the region during the Yom Kippur War.

Israel had already had experience of British tanks with the Centurion and wanted the Chieftain for its improved main armament, the 120 mm rifled gun, which was regarded at the time as 'highly accurate and world beating'. The ammunition differed from most contemporary main tank armament as it used projectiles and charges that were loaded separately, as opposed to a single fixed round. The design of the bagged charge system was initiated after an earlier liquid propellant gun project had failed due to the injection pump being so large that no tank could accommodate it. This led to design studies to find a means of reducing the ammunition size and from this the 'bagged charge concept' emerged. The charges were encased in combustible bags and these charges were stored in 36 recesses surrounded by a pressurised mixture of water and glycol known as 'wet storage'. In the event of a hit penetrating **»**

the fighting compartment, the jacket would rupture soaking the charges and preventing a catastrophic propellant explosion. As there was no shell case, the firing of the charge was by vent tubes automatically loaded from a ten-round magazine on the breech. An advantage of using two-part ammunition was that in the case of inert rounds like Armour-piercing discarding sabots (APDS) the loader could reach for the next round and hold it in his lap, ready to load while the gunner was acquiring the target and firing. This practice increased the rate of fire but would be hazardous with one-piece ammunition.

During the planning and development stages the two prototype Chieftains sent to Tel Aviv for trials had received a good reception. The gun was 21ft long and was fitted with a hydro-pneumatic recoil system using two buffers. On firing, the gun recoiled 15in and in action the crew could fire eight rounds a minute at a maximum range of 8,700 yards.

BELOW: Israeli Centurions pictured on the live fire ranges ion 1973. IDF

The length of the gun required balancing on the tank and to counter this the turret was designed with a large overhang to the rear. This contained radios, ammunition, and fire control equipment as well as additional external stowage. The gun could fire a wide range of ammunition, but the most commonly loaded types were the high explosive squash head (HESH) and the armour APDS. When first introduced, the APDS rounds were fired using a cylindrical charge. The high explosive squash head (HESH), smoke and other rounds used a hemi-cylindrical - a cylinder sliced in two lengthways – charge. The Chieftain could store up to 64 projectiles although the propellant stowage allowed a maximum of 36 charges for APDS rounds. The gun was fully stabilised with a fully computerised integrated control system. The secondary armament consisted of a coaxial 7.62mm machine gun, with a second standard general purpose machine

gun (GPMG) mounted on the commander's cupola. The Chieftain also had a nuclear, biological, and chemical protection system, which the Centurion lacked and included a simple but clever idea to install an infantry telephone fitted to the rear of the tank to facilitate communication with soldiers.

Chieftain in the Desert

The Chieftain was intended to fight Soviet armour on the plains of northern Germany, but in service with the British Army it never fired a shot in anger. Instead, it was in the heat and sand of the Middle East that the Chieftain fought its major battles during the Iran-Iraq War of the 1980s, where it proved to be very effective when in service with the Kuwaiti Army during the Gulf War of 1991. The Chieftain was sold to Kuwait, Oman, Jordan, and Iran who procured the largest foreign sale. It was used extensively by Teheran, during the Iran -Iraq war of 1980–88, including seeing service in Operation Nasr, the largest tank battle of the war. Three Iranian armoured regiments advanced towards Iraqi forces that had invaded Iranian territory between the cities of Ahvaz, Susangerd, and Dezful. The Iraqi forces were alerted to this movement and mounted a withdrawal deception plan forming three armoured brigades into a three-sided box ambush. The Iranians advanced into the trap and the two forces battled for four days in a sea of mud. The Iranians withdrew, leaving many tanks destroyed and others disabled and stuck in the mud. Others had been abandoned after running run out of fuel or ammunition.

The Chieftains performed with mixed results, some suffered from chronic engine problems and low power-to-weight-ratio – leaving the tanks struggling in the muddy terrain

and vulnerable to Iraqi fire. After the battle, Iraqis took captured Chieftains of the Iranian 92nd Armoured Division back to Baghdad for trials. At the time General Aladdin Makki, the Iraqi Army Corps chief of staff, claimed that Iraqi sabot rounds 'went through the front armour of the Chieftain and came out the backside'. There was no evidence provided to support the claim, but the highly sensitive armour used by the British was not supplied on the export versions to Iran. This, as well as the Chieftain's poor off-road capability influenced the Iraqis to reject the UK's offer to buy the Chieftain. The Iraqis claimed that in one battle the Iranian 16th Armoured Division, which was equipped with Chieftain tanks, was destroyed by the 10th Iraqi Armoured Brigade, in just 12 hours. The Iraqis were armed with T-72 tanks, but obviously much smaller in number as a brigade.

In 2024, the exported Chieftains, renamed 'Mobarez' that survived the war with Iraq are still in service with Iran. The Chieftain also saw combat when Saddam Hussein's forces invaded Kuwait in August 1990. On the eve of the Iraqi invasion Kuwait had 143 Chieftains in service. As Iraqi tanks poured into the Gulf state a total of 37 Chieftains of the 35th Armoured Brigade fought Saddam's forces in a conflict known as the Battle of the Bridges. They fought the Iraqi Hammurabi and Medina divisions in a delaying action before withdrawing over the Saudi border. The Kuwaitis though failed to block the Mutla Pass and were ineffective at delaying the Iraqis and withdrew into the desert and joined the Joint Command Forces East task force of the Coalition. After the liberation of Kuwait, the ageing Chieftains were replaced by the Yugoslav M-84.

A number of variants of the Chieftain were produced including the Armoured Recovery Vehicle (ARV), Armoured Recovery and Repair Vehicle (ARRV), the Armoured Vehicle laying bridge (AVLB) and the Chieftain Armoured Vehicle Royal Engineers (CHAVRE). The CHAVRE could also carry a fascine – a bundle of plastic pipes used to fill ditches or trenches - and tow the Python, a mine clearing charge that was fired ahead of the tank. The Chieftain tank continued to be upgraded in protection and mobility throughout the 1980s and 90s as planners shaped the tank's replacement – the Challenger.

In December 1988, the then UK defence secretary George Younger made a statement to the House of Commons about the replacement of Chieftain, saying: "Chieftain entered service with the British Army in 1965. Although it continues to give excellent service, it is now rather advanced in years, and technology in this field has moved ahead. It has proved impracticable to organise an international collaborative tank project in an early time scale. Allied collaboration in tanks and their armament remains an important objective for the future; but I have concluded that Chieftain must be replaced as soon as practicable by a tank developed nationally by this country or an ally. I have also decided, subject to satisfactory contractual terms, to upgrade the armament of the Challenger 1 tanks now in service by fitting them with an improved gun." Britain's main battle tank for 20 years, Chieftain was one of the first true MBTs, designed to replace both medium and heavy tanks in front line service. The last British regiment equipped with Chieftains was the 1st Royal Tank Regiment.

ABOVE: Iranian Chieftains shortly after Teheran purchased the tanks from the UK. ISN

BELOW: Chieftains in the Omani desert in the late 1970s. MoD

»

THE CHIEFTAIN MBT FV4201

ABOVE: The Chieftain was a development of the Centurion and was used by the British Army from the 1960s to the 1990s, with the Mark 5 serving throughout the 1970s. Tank Encyclopedia

RIGHT: The Chieftain main battle tank during training at Bovington. MoD

The Chieftain was one of the first true main battle tanks, designed to replace both medium and heavy tanks in front line service. When it came into service in the 1960s it was the heaviest and most powerful platform in NATO. The original design of the Chieftain tank called for a petrol 'V8 Rolls Royce engine' – on the basis of reliability and engineering excellence. A decision was taken to drop the V8 and go with a yet to be produced multi fuel engine, which would allow the Chieftain to run on diesel or any grade of petrol. The reason for this being that NATO commanders had suggested that in a future conflict there could be a shortage of diesel fuel – the UK was the only country in the alliance to act on the warning. The Leyland L-60 engine was, on paper, an ideal replacement for the Rolls Royce in the Chieftain. While the planning weight was 45 tonnes, the extra armour pushed the weight to 55 tonnes and not surprisingly caused challenges for the engine and transmission in a series of technical problems when the tank was first rolled out. Crews claimed the tank was underpowered and clouds of

RIGHT: The Chieftain gun barrel. DPL

engine smoke risked giving away the tanks' position when the vehicles were on manoeuvres. These problems included cylinder liner failure, fan drive problems and perpetual leaks due to vibration and badly routed pipework. However, breakdowns were gradually ironed out as improvements were introduced.

The commander of a Chieftain, even when closed down, had a good all-round field of vision through periscopes mounted around the top of the cupola. To his left he had the commander's firing control while directly to his front a fixed binocular sight allowed him to view the gun direction. To his right a small map light was fitted, and many thought the commander also had the best seat in the tank, it was hydraulic and when the tank was travelling and the hatch open, he could elevate his position so if needed he could sit with his head out of the turret. The grip switch also allowed the commander to have total control of the main gun. He could fire the General-Purpose Machine Gun (GPMG) manually when his hatch was open or by remote control when closed down. In front and below of the commander was the gunner's station – a very uncomfortable one. It was smallest position in the tank sat below the commander. The gunner had a firing control and the ability to manually control the main armament. The gunner also has the responsibility of firing the multi barrel smoke dischargers.

The last position in the turret was the loader, who had more room than any other member of the crew. As well as being in charge of the ammunition, the loader was also the tank's radio operator and tea maker. A small grey box, called the boiling vessel was situated to the loader's left. This allowed water to be boiled to make a cup of tea and also heat the 'boil in the bag' rations which the crew was issued with. As well as 64 rounds of tank ammunition, more than 6,000 rounds of linked 7.62mm ammunition were also stored. They were automatically fed to the guns on the cupola. The driver's compartment was small, and a tall soldier simply would not get into the seat. He steered by use of conventional tillers to the left and right of his legs. The driver's cab is regarded as 'very comfortable' by those who have driven the Chieftain, but climbing down into the small space and then being locked in by the heavy hatch is not for everyone. The design of the driver's seat required him to wind his chair back when locked down and lay semi-recumbent, like a dentist's chair, which helped to reduce the profile of the forward glacis plate. Tall soldiers need not apply for his post as there simply is not room.

CHIEFTAIN (FV 4201) MAIN BATTLE TANK SPECIFICATION

Model	Chieftain
Manufacturer	Leyland Motors
Country	United Kingdom
Year	1960s–90s
Engine	Leyland L60 multi-fuel two-stroke opposed piston compression ignition. 750hp
Fuel	Diesel
Protection	Glacis: 127mm
Top Speed	25mph (40kph)
Range	310 miles (498km)
Crew Capacity	Four
Length	35ft
Width	12ft
Height	10ft
Armament	L11A5 120mm rifled gun
Weight	55 tonnes
Service Branch	British Army

LEFT: In Germany during the Cold War the Chieftain was painted with block squares for urban warfare. MoD

BELOW: The Chieftain during trials in Germany pictured alongside an early Leopard. Mod

EUROPEAN TANKS

On opposite sides through two world wars to become Western allies, European militaries have had a huge influence on the tank and tank tactics.

Europe's Innovations

For decades Europe has been at the centre of tank development with Germany setting the pace for both innovative design and armoured technology with their Leopard main battle tank. During the Cold War, tanks were seen as a priority to block any Soviet aspirations to move armour into West Germany. Many countries on the continent purchased American tanks which had been mass produced and widely available after the war. During the 1960s, '70s, and '80s, the Cold War years, the fields of NATO countries were regularly packed with US Army M48s, the British Chieftain, and the French AMX-30 main battle tanks, deployed on military exercises. They were at readiness to defend against the mass armoured divisions of Moscow and the Warsaw Pact, the latter having been created in 1955 in response to ››

BELOW: Leopard tanks take part in a chemical warfare exercise. NATO

ABOVE: Sweden's Strv 122 is a variant of the German Leopard. Swedish MoD

LEFT: Germany's Leopard main battle tank has become a clear favourite with European nations. NATO

BELOW: Sweden's unique Strv 103 has an ultra-low profile. Swedish MoD

the formation of the NATO Alliance. At that time the Warsaw Pact included Albania, Bulgaria, Czechoslovakia, East Germany, Hungary, Poland, and Romania, who combined could field more than 30,700 tanks compared to just 16,000 by the nations of France, Luxembourg, the Netherlands, Belgium, Norway, Britain, the United States, and Denmark. Sweden developed its own tank, the Stridsvagn which, having been heavily upgraded

remains in service. It was developed in the post war years and remains in service. It has incredibly low profile for its three crew.

By 1955 West Germany, Portugal, Turkey, and Greece had joined NATO. Then after years of political tension the collapse of the Soviet Union saw a change in political and military thinking which forced Eastern Bloc nations took look to the West. The Czech Republic, Poland,

and Hungary were among the first to join NATO and by the early 2000s the Alliance had a membership of 32 nations. This period of history saw incursions, revolutions, and small wars across the continent. The Yugoslav wars saw the deployment of main battle tanks, as did the the so-called ten-day war in Slovenia when the country declared independence from Yugoslavia. The Bosnian war saw sustained fighting

ABOVE: The French Leclerc has been in service since 1992 and is due to be upgraded or replaced.
French Govt

BELOW: Britain's Challenger came into service in the 1980s but did not attract sales in Europe.
Jack Williams/DPL

LEFT: A Serbian T-72 in Kosovo – war came to the region in the 1990s.
Yves DeBay/DPL

in central Europe in a politically and regionally complicated conflict in which the Serbian Army fielded more than 200 tanks – many of them Soviet era T-55 platforms. As the violence flared in central Europe, America, Denmark, Norway, France, and Britain deployed main battle tanks as part of the United Nations Protection Force (UNPROFOR) in a peacekeeping role. The UK's Challenger tanks arrived on January 10, 1996 in support of the peace accord and were based in northwest Bosnia. In 1999 NATO tanks were deployed into Kosovo as part of a peace keeping task force as the country sought to break away from Serbia.

The return of high-intensity war on the European continent in »

LEFT: A Danish Leopard tank on peacekeeping duty in Bosnia. NATO

BELOW: Norway selected the Leopard tank for its off-road capability and performance in cold climates. NATO

Ukraine has revived interest in the role and future relevance of the main battle tank (MBT). In 2023 armoured units from the Alliance deployed to Norway and Finland as part of a reinforcement exercise in the wake of Russian aggression.

War in Europe

NATO's first deployment of tanks in Europe took place in the 1990s when main battle tanks were sent into Bosnia to oversee and maintain the Dayton Peace Agreement. Britain, France, the US, and others reluctantly deployed tanks onto European soil to oversee the end of the war. Moscow expressed support for the Serbs, but after years of fighting agreed with the West to a peace solution. Then, in 1999 Kosovo declared its intention to become independent and fighting

erupted between Albanians and the Serbs. NATO sent in a peace force to maintain stability and protect the Albanians and without any

announcement the Russians also arrived in tanks and armoured vehicles. As the British raced to secure the airport at Pristina, Moscow's paratroopers also arrived. In driving rain neither side was prepared to back down and Russian tanks arrived to reinforce their position. Challenger tanks stood nearby as the tension soared with NATO's senior commander demanding the Russians leave. Eventually an agreement was reached and the Russians controlled one half of the airfield and NATO the other. It had been a 'difficult moment'; which one senior British General described as 'a situation that could easily have deteriorated into something ugly'. It was the first and last time that NATO had

ABOVE: Poland has gifted many of its Leopard tanks to Ukraine. NATO

RIGHT: Poland is to replace its Leopards with Abrams. NATO

been the 'national security' factor of design and innovation which governments have been reluctant to share, and the economic priority of maintaining highly skilled workers to build the platforms. The United States dipped its toe into the 'joint venture' world with Germany in the 1970s but pressure to build in the US and maintain American technology and jobs was overriding. Ironically, one of NATO's drivers has been for commonality to reduce pressure on the logistics of re-supply. But while efforts have been made to standardise ammunition and many other items, the tank has in the main avoided a single design that streamlines components. Washington is currently reviewing options for a future tank with the AbramsX being proposed as the next generation US platform. In 2020, Poland developed a light concept tank with a low profile, called the PL-01. It will, if commissioned, incorporate reactive armour and a powerful 120mm gun. Conflict in eastern Europe has raised the importance of the tank and ended the drought across NATO in tank investment. It has again highlighted the difficulty in operating numerous variants of tank which increases pressure on the logistics supply chain, as well as the specialist mechanics needed to maintain these platforms. It is this need for 'standard parts' which was adopted by many European car manufacturers in the early 21st century. In April 2024 defence ministers of France and Germany met in Paris to ratify an agreement on a new joint tank project called the Main Ground Combat System (MGCS). This project launched in 2017 is aimed at replacing Germany's Leopard 2 and the French Leclerc by 2040. The overall aim is to reduce costs with commonality of parts and weapons systems while embracing the best capabilities from each country. The project has attracted wide interest with Norway, Spain, »

worked with Russian forces. As the operation in Kosovo continued NATO tanks patrolled the streets and mounted reassurance exercises in areas where Albanian communities felt threatened.

Future European Tank

Tanks are an expensive 'deterrent' held in readiness to support peacekeeping or warfighting. Since the end of the Cold War the status of the main battle tank became relegated as Europe enjoyed relative peace. Commanders called for more investment to avoid a low state of readiness and increasingly governments have looked to buy 'off the shelf' ready to use tanks from the United States or more often from Germany. Main battle tanks (MBTs) have been around for just over 100 years and during that period they have been continuously evolving with improved firepower, survivability, and mobility. But there have been few new designs – instead the trend has been to upgrade existing platforms rather than develop or purchase new ones. Since 2000, the

number of MBTs in EU member states has decreased, from 15,000 to just 5,000 in 2024. Many countries facing fiscal challenges are reducing the numbers of platforms with the UK being one example. In the 1990s the UK's armoured force numbered more the 900 tanks, in 2020 it was down to 227, and the current Challenger 3 upgrade will see just 148 tanks modified and kept in service. The challenge for Europe has

RIGHT: The French government has entered a joint venture with Germany to build a new European tank. NATO

ABOVE: Poland's futuristic tank the PL-01 – a concept for a future European tank.
Polish MoD

Poland, and Sweden- who all use Leopard tanks – expressing an interest to join the project, as well as Italy and the UK who field their own indigenous tanks.

But even Europe's MGCS appears to be reinventing the wheel. The business behind the project, the European defence company KNDS, unveiled in 2022 what was described as the Enhanced Main Battle Tank (EMBT), based on a heavily modified Leopard 2 hull. The tank will carry a 120mm smoothbore gun fed by a bustle-mounted autoloader with 22 ready rounds of ammunition. In terms of secondary armament, EMBT was provided with a 12.7mm coaxial heavy machine gun (HMG) with 680 ready rounds, as well as a combined commander's panoramic sight and remote weapon station (RWS) armed with a 7.62mm machine gun (MG) with 800 ready rounds. While the weapons system seems very similar to those currently deployed, it is the shape of the new European tank that will be distinctively different. Sharp slopes and an angled turret will give it a space-like profile.

The MGCS will also be supported by unmanned ground vehicles (UGVs) which the tank crew will be able to deploy ahead of its position. The UGVs will deliver reconnaissance and surveillance, provide a mine clearing and IED capability as well as delivering a chemical testing resource in case of biological attacks. The joint venture is designed to balance costs while nations will have the ability to fit their own armour. Weight as always is the growing problem; planners estimated the new European tank will weigh 61 tonnes while the UK's new Challenger is expected to be in excess of 67 tonnes.

RIGHT: The Leopard is renowned for its speed and manoeuvrability.
NATO

Leopard at War

After Putin's invasion of Ukraine, several NATO nations donated Leopard tanks to support President Zelensky's war effort. The German government debated the plan and eventually decided to send a batch of refurbished Leopard main battle tanks to Ukraine. In total Berlin agreed to NATO nations sending 80 Leopard 1 and 80 advanced Leopard 2 tanks. Since their arrival at least 12 Leopards have been destroyed. Mines and drones have accounted for most of the German-made Leopard 2s the Ukrainian army have lost. But as well as mines, drones, and artillery, the Russians have used multiple RPG strikes to disable Leopard tanks. In one incident witnessed by Ukrainian commanders a projectile was fired into the side of a 2000-era Leopard - which has thicker armour and a longer, more powerful gun than older Leopard 2 variants have. The attack involved more than six RPGs striking the tanks at the same time and it quickly caught fire. The German tank remains one of the most powerful vehicles in Europe and while the upgrades have delivered more protection and firepower, there is no sign that this great Leopard is about to change its spots.

Leopard

The Leopard 1 was powered by a liquid cooled, supercharged diesel engine. This ten-cylinder engine with multi-fuel capability is typically run-on diesel fuel (NATO designation F-54). The Leopard 1's hull was fabricated from welded armoured plate of varying thickness - while the turret was a complex all-cast component. Crew protection was enhanced with an automatic, and manual trigger, fire suppression system and an NBC protection system, which produces an overpressure in the crew compartment to provide filtration of air. The Leopard 1 has had, and continues to have on upgraded tanks, a remarkable fording capability and can cross waterways without any prior preparation. Deep rivers, more than eight feet can be crossed by sealing the tank and fitting a foldable snorkel over the commander's cupola - two bilge pumps are provided to remove any water accumulation. The Leopard 1 had a conventional layout adopted in many post-war tanks with the driver at the front, the commander and gunner in the right of the turret with the loader to the left. The engine compartment was separated from the crew with

added metal-rubber skirts along the hull flanks to protect against HEAT warheads, and the gun barrel was wrapped in a jacket to reduce deviation from thermal loads. The track was changed to a double-pin type with detachable, rectangular rubber pads. The rubber pads of the new tracks could be easily replaced with metal X-shaped grousers for movement on ice on and snow. A new snorkel was developed that allowed for underwater driving to a depth of 4m after sealing the tank with special plugs. The driver's and commander's active infrared night vision periscopes were replaced with passive image intensification night sights. By 1977 all of the tanks in the first four batches of Leopard 1 were upgraded. Additional turret armour was also added which consisted of rubber-lined steel plates bolted to the turret with shock-resistant spacers. The gun mantlet received a wedge-shaped armoured cover made from welded steel plates and the engine's air intake system was improved. The upgraded vehicles weighed 42.4 tonnes. More upgrades took place in the 1960s and 70s prior to the development of the Leopard 2 which was designed with a new shaped turret. The tank first entered service in 1979, and its service life is anticipated to end around 2030. »

LEFT: A Leopard 2 pictured in Germany on manoeuvres with NATO forces. IDF

LEFT: The tank has maintained its position as mainland Europe's top tank since it entered service. NATO

a fireproof bulkhead. There have been suggestions that the initial armour was just 2.75in on the front and even less on the turret. The initial Leopard 1 was capable of sustained road speeds of 40mph and had a range of 372 miles. From a maintenance and repair point of view the engine was designed so that it could be lifted out and replaced in the field within 20 minutes. The principle has been maintained on the Leopard 2. This was a major improvement from the high maintenance that crews endured on the Tiger tank. In 1970 the German

defence ministry commissioned an upgrade programme to increase the combat effectiveness of the tank. Known as the Leopard A1. This overhaul saw the addition of

LEFT: A Leopard 2 crashes through water during a training exercise in Germany. NATO

BELOW: Live firing on the ranges by a pair of Leopards. NATO

THE LEOPARD

The German Leopard main battle tank was originally developed and built in the late 1960s and is widely regarded as a super tank. Designed by the car manufacturer Porsche, this fine example of German engineering offered speed, protection and a deep wading capability that allows the tank, when fitted with a snorkel, to cross almost any waterway.

The tank was widely regarded as the best of its kind in the world, combining both speed and accuracy. Ironically, the Leopard 1 tanks were initially fitted with a British 105mm L7 gun, an armament that had been fitted on the Centurion. The finished German tank weighed just 40 tonnes and delivered fantastic cross-country performance.

Its reputation quickly resulted in foreign armies queuing up to purchase export variants when it was complete. Since 1965, more than 4,700 units of the Leopard 1 have been produced and remain in use in nine countries.

ABOVE: Designed by Porsche and first entering service in the mid-1960s, this model is used by several armies across Europe, as well as countries as far afield as Canada and Australia. Tank Encyclopedia

RIGHT: The Leopard 1 main battle tank in service with the Norwegian Army. NATO

BELOW: A Leopard 1 pictured taking part in European wargames during the Cold War. NATO

Continuous updates have ensured that today the Leopard 2 continues to deliver state of the art capability.

The evolution of the Leopard 1 tank dates to the late 1950s, when West Germany, along with its NATO partners, recognised the requirement

for a new main battle tank to counter the growing military threat from the Soviet Union's T-54 and T-55 tanks at a time of high Cold War tension between the West and Moscow. In 1956, Germany initiated a joint project with France, and Italy, which it named

the Euro panzer project. The aim was to create a standard tank within the alliance. France was very interested in the design as its planned AMX-50 had stalled and in the summer of 1957 Berlin and Paris signed an agreement to develop a joint tank.

The Germans provided three designs and the French one with prototypes being produced. In late 1958 Italy joined the venture and in 1960 testing began on a tank designed by Porsche. The second from Rheinmetall and a third, futuristic design from Borgward, who were based in Bremen – however, they failed to have a prototype ready in time. In 1963, the Porsche prototype was eventually selected as the winner of the contest. The announcement did not come as a surprise as two years earlier it had already been decided to build a pre-series of 50 vehicles based on the Porsche design.

Germany dropped France from the joint programme after a series of missed deadlines and in July 1963 the German Defence Ministry ordered 1,500 tanks with production to take

place between 1965 and 1970 – the initial vehicle weighed 40 tonnes and the unit cost was estimated at £270,000 per tank.

Leopard production started in 1964 and the tank entered service in 1966. It was deemed so good that Belgium, the Netherlands, Norway, Italy, Denmark, Australia, Canada, Turkey, and Greece all purchased the tank. Spain and Chile later ordered the Leopard but at the time they were

under dictatorships and Germany declined to sell to them – so they purchased the French AMX-30 instead.

In the mid-1960s, Germany announced it had entered a joint venture with the United States to develop a future tank for both nations. Called the MBT-70, The programme faced significant challenges from the start, including poor communication and coordination between the American and West German teams working on the project. The US military and the German defence ministry had requirements which were not aligned, and they were not resolved before the project was too far advanced to be changed. By the late 1960s, the development of the MBT-70 was well over budget, leading West Germany to withdraw from the project in 1969. The US continued development of the MBT-70 until 1971 when the programme was finally cancelled, with funds and technology from the MBT-70 project redirected to the development of the M1 Abrams. Meanwhile, West Germany opted to develop its own new tank and worked on a project which was later unveiled as the Leopard.

ABOVE: The Leopard tank can wade and swim through water up to four metres deep. NATO

LEFT: An early Leopard 1 pictured during wargames in late 1950s. NATO

BELOW LEFT: A Leopard I on manoeuvres in central Europe during the Cold War. NATO

BELOW: A convoy of Leopard 1s. NATO

TANKS OF THE GULF WAR

War in the Middle East put the tank firmly back in the defence spotlight.

Coalition Armour

The Gulf War was a major conflict in the Middle East which took place after Iraq invaded Kuwait in August 1990 and Saddam Hussein refused to withdraw. The Arab states joined a US led coalition and in 1991 mounted an operation, headed by tanks to eject the invaders by force.

The United States deployed the Abrams, France sent the AMX-30, while Britain mobilised two armoured brigades of Challenger tanks. While many regional Gulf nations contributed troops, it was mainly Egypt, Syria, Saudi Arabi, and exiled Kuwaiti forces who deployed armour. The Kuwaiti Army consisted of four brigades, with over 140 Chieftain and M-84 tanks. The biggest Arab contingent came from Egypt who deployed hundreds of M60 tanks, while Syria committed more than 150 T-62 tanks. The Saudi force included the 10th Armoured Brigade and the 8th, 10th, 11th, and 20th Mechanised Brigades equipped with 550 French AMX-30s and US M60s. In the late 1970s, Saudi Arabia had reinforced its armoured capability with more than 900 M60 main battle tanks, many of them were upgraded M60s. Then, in 1990 Saudi Arabia inspected and purchased 390 newer M60A3s from US redundant resources. The Saudi tank crews were trained by the US Army and the 50 tonne armoured platforms were quickly integrated across the force.

The Royal Saudi Army initially deployed several hundred tanks,

which they later increased and operated throughout with the US Marines. Many of the Saudi M60s saw action as part of the coalition force and participated in the Battle of Khafji, the first major ground engagement of the conflict. Qatar also provided an armoured battalion equipped with 24 French-supplied AMX-30 tanks, while Bahrain sent a brigade supported with M60A main battle tanks. The Sultan of Oman sent a battalion of infantry and a

small number of Scimitar armoured reconnaissance vehicles.

In total, the coalition gathered half a million men from 31 countries armed with 3,400 tanks and an estimated 9,000 armoured vehicles. Britain's Challenger main battle tank, affectionately known as the 'Chally', faced its combat 'baptism of fire' in the Gulf War when the UK's armoured brigade deployed as part the coalition. The Challenger design and concept had originated ❯❯

LEFT: An Egyptian M60 tank crew in Saudi Arabia. Cairo deployed significant numbers of tanks to support the coalition. MoD

BELOW: During the campaign to oust Iraqi forces from Kuwait, Saudi Arabia deployed the American-built M60 in large numbers. DPL

in a planned Iranian order for an improved version of the Chieftain which Teheran had purchased. The former military engineering establishment in Surrey had pioneered the project, but with the fall of the Shah of Iran, the tank order collapsed, and the design was re-directed towards the European Market. The British Army viewed the project as a replacement for the Chieftain, which at the time was being explored in a venture called Main Battle Tank -80 (MBT-80). By the early 1980s the Challenger was in service and in 1991 the tank was poised to move into the desert.

The Kuwaiti Army had been taken by surprise in 1990, despite all the warnings and threats from Baghdad. Prior to the Iraqi invasion, Kuwait's armoured holdings included 70 old British Vickers Mk1 tanks, and 40 Centurions. Both were in the process of being withdrawn from service and were replaced with 165 Chieftain MBTs and a smaller number of Yugoslavian built M-84s. By August 1990 the majority of Challengers had been delivered but only a small number of the M-84s had arrived. In addition, more than 200 Soviet T-72s built under licence were still on order but not delivered. Kuwaiti forces resisted the Iraq assault but were vastly outnumbered. The 35th Armoured Brigade fought a delaying action near Al Jahra, west of Kuwait City, while in the south, the 15th Armoured Brigade moved

immediately to evacuate its forces to Saudi Arabia.

In the late 1980s the Egyptian Army had procured hundreds of M60 tanks from the United States and in 1990 the government in Cairo was one of the first Arab nations to step forward and offer support to Kuwait when Iraq invaded. Egypt sent more than 35,000 troops and several hundred tanks to Saudi Arabia in support of Operation Desert Storm. It was the second largest contingent, after the US, and Egypt was a key Arab partner in the 28-nation coalition against Iraq. Egyptian M60 tanks joined Kuwaiti forces in the spearhead of the coalition ground offensive against Iraq. The tanks were issued first to the two independent tank brigades and then to the 4th and 9th Armoured Divisions. Outside the US, the Egyptian Army had one of the biggest M60 forces. In 1990 the Egyptian tanks were loaded aboard ships and ferried to Saudi, and the Egyptian armoured force was among the first to enter Kuwait.

Syria had a long relationship with Czechoslovak arms factories and

in the early 1990s purchased the T-62 tank . It was re-graded as a revolutionary tank at the time with excellent armour protection, good manoeuvrability, and gun. When it was first produced in 1961 it was regarded the best main battle tank in the world but was quickly overtaken. The T-62 design was very low to the ground and this low profile meant they were harder to hit. Syria deployed 14,500 troops and more than 150 hundred tanks to the region as part of the coalition. »

ABOVE: A Saudi M60 deployed on operations during the 1991 conflict. US DoD

LEFT: Syria deployed large numbers of T-55 tanks as part of the coalition to oust Iraq from Kuwait. US DoD

BELOW: A Kuwaiti M-84 in the desert during the 1991 Gulf War. Yves DeBay

Baghdad's Armoured Force

In the 1991 Gulf War, Iraq's powerful T-72 tank force was a significant concern to coalition commanders. Saddam's armoured divisions had fought an eight-year war against Iran and intelligence reports indicated the Republican Guard was well drilled in 'manoeuvre warfare' – a tactic of outflanking an enemy - which Baghdad's forces had used to inflict heavy losses on the Iranians. Among the Iraqi arsenal was a small number of 'home produced' T-72M1s – a variant built by Iraq and dubbed the 'Lions of Babylon' by the media. However, it turned out that these 'lions' and indeed most of Iraq's main battle tanks had no teeth, at least when pitted against American M1A1 Abrams, the British Challenger, the French AMX-30 and even the older US M-60A3s. During the 1991 conflict many T-72s crews failed to use their manoeuvrability and instead dug their tanks into fixed defensive positions in the desert – making them easy targets for coalition tanks who moved across the desert at speed to flank the Iraqi force. There is no question that in 1990 when Saddam's forces invaded Kuwait the Iraqi Army was well resourced and capable. But while Baghdad could field numerous variants of main battle tanks, armoured personnel carriers, and reconnaissance vehicles, there appeared to be little inter-operability between vehicle types and weapon systems. This made repair and re-supply a challenge with so many

different spares needed to support the force. As Iraq faced conflict in 1991 the army was able to field five different main battle tanks and more than 15 armoured vehicles, compared to two tanks among US forces and one among British and French, as well as a couple of different armoured vehicles. Unlike Western forces who invested in one or two vehicle variants, Iraq fielded French, Soviet, Brazilian, Chinese, and Yugoslavian armoured vehicles which offered very little commonality. This put strain on the army's service support and ability to repair and maintain vehicles and may well have been Baghdad's 'Achilles' heel' forcing many tanks to sit in the sands due to maintenance issues.

The Soviet-designed T-72 main battle tank served as the backbone of the Iraqi armoured forces during

the Iran conflict and the following 1990-1991 Gulf War. Developed in the 1960s, the T-72 was known for its battlefield capability, its powerful 125mm smoothbore gun, and composite armour. Iraq acquired a substantial number of T-72 tanks from the Soviet Union in the 1970s and 1980s. Compared to main battle tanks used in the West, the T-72 has a much smaller profile and is lighter at 41 tonnes. It was highly manoeuvrable and could traverse rivers using an installed snorkel allowing the entire tank to submerge.

For submerged operations each member of the crew is equipped with a basic chest-pack rebreather in case of emergency. But if the tank flooded it must have been a terrifying situation. The T-72's engine compartment can flood from pressure loss and if the engine stops

ABOVE: Iraqi T-72 tanks had a good reputation but many of them had not been maintained. US DoD

BELOW: An Iraqi T-72 caught in the open by coalition tanks. US DoD

ABOVE: Many of Iraq's Iraqi T-62 were held in reserve south of Baghdad. US DoD

RIGHT: T-62s could generate a smokescreen - a classic Soviet tactic. US DoD

underwater, it must be started again within six seconds. The limited space made escape challenging and 'submerge' training exercises were not popular. The tank was also nuclear, biological, and chemical (NBC) capable – providing a clean air environment for the crew in time of attack.

Iraq's armoured brigades also included large numbers of T-62s, but in 1991 these tanks lacked high powered optics, thermal sights and basic computer technology compared to their adversaries. The Iraqi's 3rd Armored Division alone lost 110 of their T-62 tank force. The T-62 medium tank, known under

the Soviet identification of Object 166 officially entered service in the Soviet Army in August 1961. It was designed and built at Factory No.183 in Nizhniy Tagil, known as Uralvagonzavod. The vehicle was developed as a direct response to the then new American M60 tank, which had been dispatched to the 3rd Armored Division to serve with the US Army in Europe in December 1960. The design of the T-62 was an amalgamation of several existing concepts which had previously remained at the experimental stage, but nevertheless were already well established before the M60 was known in the USSR.

But had not been built. In addition to the research work that had been accumulated since the start of a new Soviet medium tank programme in 1953, several more years were spent in shaping the T-62 into its final design. Many components, from communications to lighting, were adopted as standard from previous tanks.

The crew of a T-62 was equipped with the same controls and observation devices as those used in their T-55 counterparts. The driver was provided with two periscopes, laid out to ensure that he could see both front corners of the hull. He could swap out one periscope for a night-vision periscope, which could also be mounted externally when driving from an open hatch. The loader had a single rotating periscope for a relatively restricted view to the left side of the turret. The gunner was provided with a single forward-facing periscope for general observation and to alleviate sickness which could be a problem when the tank was locked down and the gunner had no vision. His main observation device was a telescopic sight, known as the TSh2B-41. The on-board fuel carried in a T-62 was divided between four internal Bakelite-coated steel tanks, holding a total of 148 gallons, and three external tanks on the fenders with a capacity of 60 gallons. Additionally, a pair of external fuel drums could be mounted onto the rear of the hull for extended range – a tactic used on many Soviet tanks.

The T-62 was the first production tank equipped with a smoothbore **»**

tank gun that could fire armour piercing stabilised rounds at a greater velocity than earlier tanks, which has used rifled tank guns. Due to its greater manufacturing costs and maintenance requirements than its predecessor, the T-62 did not completely replace the T-55 in export markets, even though it became the standard tank in the Soviet arsenal. Inside the T-62 space is at a premium. The driver's compartment is in the lower front, the fighting compartment in the middle, and the engine compartment at the rear. The loader, gunner, driver, and commander made up the crew of four. The tank had capacity to carry 40 'immediate use' rounds with additional rounds being kept in storage in the front of the hull, to the right of the driver, and in the rear of the fighting compartment. On operations, four rounds are kept in the turret. The coaxial machine gun's 2,500 rounds are also stored inside. The T-62 was less manoeuvrable than the T-55 because of its increased weight.

After the war with Iran, Saddam boosted his armoured capability by importing nearly 3,000 Chinese tanks instead of relying on the USSR. And, by the start of the Gulf War, the T-62 had lost much of its prominence in the Iraqi Army, making up less than a sixth of its tank fleet, but nevertheless, it took part in the fight against coalition forces in 1991. Its performance was poor, like the T-72 it appeared to have lacked maintenance while its crews' lacked motivation

and many quickly surrendered. Saddam's Army also fielded hundreds of T-55 tanks which were assigned to the 10th and 12th Armored Divisions. These tanks had spearheaded the invasion of Kuwait and in January and February of 1991, Iraqi T-55s were deployed in the desert to counter any coalition breakout. However, they lacked heavy armour which left

the crews vulnerable and when the T-55s were in action against the more advanced coalition tanks they faced formidable challenges. The coalition was able to effectively engage and destroy Iraqi T-55 tanks because they possessed sophisticated armament, including thermal imaging systems, precision-guided munitions, and better reconnaissance capabilities.

The T-55 was one of the most extensively manufactured tanks of the Cold War era. It entered service in the late 1940s and was widely deployed in the post war years. Its primary weapon was a 100mm gun, listed as the D-10T-TS2. It is capable of firing high-explosive, armour-piercing, and shaped-charge ammunition, with a maximum indirect fire mission range of 14,600 metres. To the right side of the main gun is a 7.62mm SGMT coaxial machine gun, while the driver can fire a remote-controlled weapon positioned in the middle of the glacis plate by pressing a button on the right steering lever. The driver is located in the front, the combat compartment is in the middle, and the engine and gearbox are located in the back of the T-55's all-welded steel hull. A single piece hatch that swings to the left is provided for the driver, at the front of the tank.

In front of this hatch are two-day periscopes, one of which may be switched out for an infrared periscope, which is used in tandem with the infrared light that is fixed on the right side of the glacial plate. There is a turntable in the combat compartment to compensate for the lack of space. The Iraqi T-55s lacked engine upgrades that Soviet tanks had benefited from reducing its capability.

The Iraqi force also included a first-generation Chinese main battle tank, the Type 69. The People's Republic of China supplied Iraq with more than 1,500 Type 69 MBTs in the 1980s which the Iraqi Army designated as Type 69-QM. The Iraqi Type 69-QM was fitted with a 100mm rifled gun as standard and a secondary coaxial machine gun along with a 12.7mm anti-aircraft machine gun. During the Gulf War in 1991, Iraqi Type 69 units were said to have performed well and appeared to have been maintained. There was little visual difference between the Type 59 and Type 69. The gun's fume extractor was repositioned a little, and the turret was fitted with a sizable infrared light. It was the first Chinese tank that could fight at night using a tiny infrared light on the commander's hatch and a laser rangefinder on the gun mantlet – the armoured plate to the side of the gun. It was the first tank in China to be equipped with a 100mm smoothbore gun – allowing it to fire armour-piercing, fin stabilised rounds and it had a limited gun stabilisation system. Interestingly, while coalition forces feared a chemical warfare attack from Iraqi forces, the Type 59 lacked any nuclear, biological, and chemical (NBC) protection. »

ABOVE: Iraq's huge arsenal included Chinese Type 59 tanks. US DoD

BELOW: An abandoned Iraqi Type 69 tank is inspected by US troops on the battlefield. US DoD

CHALLENGER MAIN BATTLE TANK FV4030

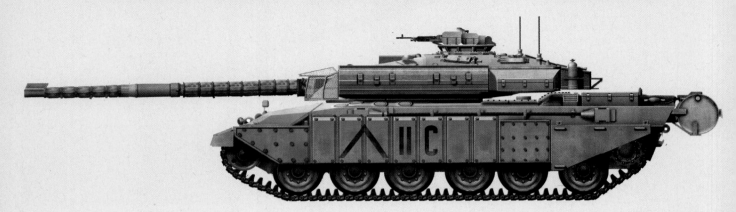

The Challenger entered service in 1983 and was an instant success. With a four-man crew, 120mm main gun, Chobham protective armour, and the ability to hit speeds of 35mph thanks to its Perkins CV12 26-litre diesel engine, the tank was regarded as innovative and revolutionary.

It was deployed to the Gulf in October 1990 as part of the 7th Armoured Brigade consisting of the Queen's Royal Hussars (QRH) and the Royal Scots Dragoon Guards (SDG) - each equipped with 57 of the latest versions of the Challenger 1. The tanks were modified for desert operations in Saudi Arabia with Chobham armour being fixed along both hulls and explosive reactive armour (ERA) on the nose and front glacis plate. Other modifications included the provision of extra external fuel drums and a smoke generator. Then, a month after the initial deployment it was decided

to send the 4th Armoured Brigade as well. This force included the 14th/20th Kings Hussars equipped with 43 more Challenger 1 tanks and reinforced by a squadron of the Life Guards which was equipped with the Mark 2 version of the tank, upgraded

by armouring the storage bins for the 120mm charges as well as the additional armour.

In early 1991 the Challenger tanks formed part of the coalition assault to remove Iraqi forces from Kuwait. The Challenger 1 saw

ABOVE: This main battle tank was used by the British Army from 1983 to 2001. During the first Gulf War more than 200 Challenger 1 tanks were operational. Tank Encyclopedia

LEFT: A force of Challenger 1 tanks pause during training in the UK. Chris Norris/DPL

BELOW: A Challenger 1 provides overwatch for coalition forces during the Gulf War. MoD

CHALLENGER 1 MAIN BATTLE TANK SPECIFICATIONS

Model	Challenger 1 FV4030 | Challenger 2 FV4034
Manufacturer	Royal Ordnance Factory
Country	United Kingdom
Year	1983–2001, subsequently upgraded to Challenger 2
Engine	Perkins CV12 26-litre diesel, 1,200hp
Fuel	Diesel
Protection	Chobham composite ceramic vehicle armour
Top Speed	35mph (60km/h)
Range	280 miles (450km)
Crew Capacity	Four including commander, gunner, loader, driver
Length	38ft
Width	12ft
Height	10ft
Armament	120mm rifled gun | 7.62mm machine guns
Weight	62 tonnes
Service Branch	British Army

RIGHT: A British Challenger crew park their tank at a road block in Pristina, Kosovo, during the 1999 NATO intervention. DPL

of the 17th/21st Lancers, attached to the Queens Royal Irish Hussars, destroyed an Iraqi T-55 tank at a range of 3,600 metres, followed soon after by a petrol tanker at a range of 4,700 metres using an armour-piercing, fin-stabilised discarding sabot (APFSDS) round. That same day, a tank of the SDGs - call sign '11 Bravo' - engaged and destroyed an Iraqi tank at a range of 5,100 metres using a L26A1 APFSDS with a depleted uranium penetrator. This is believed to be the distance record for a successful tank-on-tank, direct fire, kinetic round engagement.

direct action against Iraqi tanks, escorted vital logistics patrols, and provided flank protection for other coalition operations. On February 26, 1991, a Challenger 1 under the command of Captain Tim Purbrick

In action the Global Positioning System (GPS) and Thermal Observation and Gunnery System (TOGS) fitted to Challenger 1 proved to be decisive when engaging the enemy, allowing attacks to be made at night, in poor visibility, and through smoke screens.

During the conflict British Challengers destroyed roughly 300 Iraqi tanks without suffering a single loss in combat. In 1985, the UK Ministry of Defence had ordered a derivative armoured recovery vehicle and a number of these were sent to the Gulf to support the tank force.

RIGHT: A Challenger 2 pictured live firing. Jack Williams/DPL

TANKS OF THE MIDDLE EAST AND CHINA

As a statement of power on land, few things match the presence of a main battle tank.

BELOW: India's powerful Arjun is fitted with a 120mm main gun but it's a heavy tank with the Mark 2 hitting scales at 75 tonnes.
DRDO India

Tank Power

Tanks are a statement of influence and power which has been widely embraced by governments in the Middle East. The political importance of tanks as a signature of authority was highlighted in September 1986 when Britain's then Prime Minister Margaret Thatcher rode in the commander's position of a Challenger. With her goggles and head scarf she looked like Lawrence of Arabia as the tank raced around the British training camp at Fallingbostel in Germany. In Baghdad, after the war with Iran Saddam Hussein ordered his tank commanders to drive through the city's 'Victory Arch' and crush thousands of Iranian combat helmets – a public display to remind the population of his success. Since 1945, the Middle East has seen more conflicts involving tanks than any other region. The open desert, perfect

LEFT: Saudi Arabia has updated its armoured force with the American Abrams. US DoD

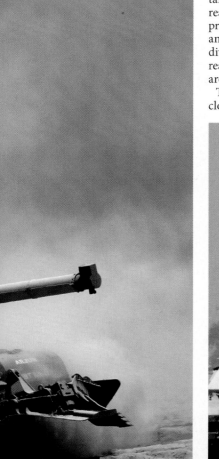

tank country, is undoubtedly a key reason why armour is given such priority. But to the east, Pakistan and India both have powerful tank divisions and maintain a high readiness in case of conflict in or around Kashmir.

The shadow of China also looms close. Beijing is resurgent and building an army of main battle tanks with an eye on Taiwan. But it is not just about power, Beijing wants to create a new world order. President Xi Jinping is a leader like no other, a commander of a powerful military and leader of a superpower he has stated that he wants China to dominate trade »

BELOW: The United States equipped Iraq with more than 300 Abrams in 2011. US DoD

in the Pacific – a challenge to Western countries. After decades in the shadows of poverty and viewing itself as a victim, Beijing is demonstrating to the world the capability of a nation that can support a powerful armoured force headed by a new Type 99A tank. The development of China's domestic third generation MBT began in 1989, alongside a naval project to build new landing ships to ferry the tank into action. The tension and potential threat of conflict between China and Taiwan should not be underestimated. Beijing views its national security as being intrinsically linked to the island and President Xi Jinping's Chinese Communist Party has stated for more than seven decades that it will secure unification.

The Middle East

Prior to the Iran -Iraq war the Middle East and Gulf region was home to more than 40,000 main battle tank tanks, the majority of Soviet vintage – today that is changing as countries across the region upgrade their main battle tanks. Egypt, Oman, Jordan, Syria, Yemen, Lebanon, and of course Israel all field tanks as frontline equipment in a region where in the past two decades conflict has never been far away.

Today, Iran operates a number of T-72 variants and still maintains a small number of Chieftains, renamed Mobarez, but it is alleged that sanctions have caused problems with access to spare parts. While Iraq has re-armed with US and Russian

tanks, Tehran announced in 2016 the development of the Karrar - despite sanctions and materials shortages. The Karrar is an upgraded T-72 main battle tank with elements of the T-90, M1 Abrams, and the Challenger 2 added – exactly what these 'elements' are is unclear. But analysts say the Iranian tank has little capability. Iraq has a new armoured force after years of reliance on ageing Soviet era armour such as the T-55, T-62, and more advanced T-72 which in the main failed Baghdad in the 1991 and 2003 wars. Today Iraq's military is equipped with modern American and Russian tanks. Following the assault into Mosul by the so-called Islamic State (ISIS) in June 2014, the United States supplied Baghdad with 320 Abrams tanks and the training to

retake the city. Then, in 2018 Moscow sold more than 70 T-90s tanks to Iraq for an undisclosed amount. The first T-90s arrived by ship at the Basra port of Umm Qasr in southern Iraq. They were transported to Baghdad and have joined a special division where they will operate alongside the Abrams.

Egypt has one of the largest and strongest armoured forces in the region with 4,393 tanks listed in its inventory, including the powerful Abrams M1A1 and many Russian types. Oman operates the UK's Challenger tank, while Jordan fields the French Leclerc. Kuwait replaced its Chieftain tanks with the Abrams and also operates Russian T-90s. Today, Saudi Arabia operates more than 900 Abrams tanks – the biggest

BELOW: Kuwait has also purchased the Abrams as some Gulf states turn to the US for their tanks. US DoD

BOTTOM: In 2016 Tehran announced the development of the Karrar - despite sanctions and materials shortages. ISN

TANK STRENGTH IN THE MIDDLE EAST	
EGYPT	4,394
SYRIA	3,540
MOROCCO	3,335
IRAN	2,831
ALGERIA	2,024
ISRAEL	1,900
JORDAN	1,401
SAUDI ARABIA	1,062)
IRAQ	826
KUWAIT	367
LEBANON	361
SUDAN	360
UAE	354
BAHRAIN	180
QATAR	134
OMAN	114

Source: Mena | Combat Tank Strength Military Trends

RIGHT: Turkey can field more than. 200 tanks, among them the South Korean K2 Black Panther. Ankara MoD

BELOW: The Egyptian government in Cairo has purchased the US Abrams. US DoD

Abrams force in the Middle East. The Riyadh force also includes a significant number of AMX-30s and retains 350 M6os. Although not sat with the Gulf region, Turkey sits in the Middle East spectrum and can field more than 2,000 main battle tanks - among them the South Korean K2 Black Panther, the Leopard 2, and the M60. Its military is regarded as highly professional and saw combat with the Leopard tank in Syria. »

The United Arab Emirates also operates the French Leclerc which it deployed to Yemen during the civil war.

Eastern Promise

China is a dominate force in the Pacific and official defence sources state that the nation has 6,457 tanks in service. Of this total, it is understood that around 1,000 are of the Type 99 model and the improved Type 99A/Type 99G variants - China's most advanced main battle tank. China is building an army of main battle tanks ready for conflict – potentially with Taiwan. Reports suggest that China is working on a futuristic fourth-generation main battle tank (MBT) which will reduce the crews to just two instead of the three currently used for the Type 99. It is understood that Beijing is planning to fit laser weapons into the new tank. It will be reduced in size to just 40-tonnes and is to be part of a high-readiness force that can be flown into action inside transport aircraft. Xi Jinping

RIGHT: China's Type 88 tanks have been in service since the late 1990s and are currently being used in the Sudan war. US DoD

BELOW: China's Type 99A main battle tank entered service in 2011 and appears to be a modern version of the Russian T-72. PLAN

has a politically stated objective to reunite Taiwan as part of China. Taiwan, the Republic of China, has an armoured force which includes the M1A2 upgraded Abrams, but the vast numbers of tanks fielded by China's People's Liberation Army Navy (PLAN) dwarfs the Taiwanese arsenal.

In May 2024 China launched its latest series of wargames in which warships and amphibious ships, packed with tanks, took part in wargames in the Taiwan Strait.

China's influence is also clear in Pakistan where most of Islamabad's tanks are Chinese or Soviet, with

the Haider MBT being the latest addition to Pakistan's indigenous tank manufacturing. Pakistan builds the VT-1A in a joint venture with Norinco of China, which is based on the Type 90-II. It has been exported to Bangladesh, Morocco, and Myanmar by China. The tank was the result of a close collaboration with China – an indication of Beijing's aim to spread its military influence. It is armed with an automatically loaded 125mm smoothbore gun and a 7.62mm co-axial machine gun (MG) mounted in its two-person turret. A remotely operated weapon system (ROWS) is also mounted on the turret roof behind the commander's position. This ROWS is armed with a 12.7mm MG fed from an ammunition stowage box mounted on the left side of its cradle. Both the gunner and commander have access to stabilised sights containing thermal imagers, enabling hunter-killer target engagement. Pakistan states that it has more than 3,000 tanks in service while India claims to field more than »

ABOVE: The Pakistani T-80 is a Soviet era design platform that was made in Ukraine. Pakistan MoD

LEFT: China's Type 96 is old but still very capable and Beijing has hundreds of these main battle tanks. PLAN

BELOW: Pakistan has a joint venture with China's Norinco company and produced MBT 200, seen here in service with Bangladesh. Pakistan MoD

4,000 including its first indigenous main battle tank, the Arjun. The Arjun features a 120mm rifled main gun with indigenously developed armour piercing, fin stabilised, discarding sabot ammunition.

Conflict in Middle East

The Middle East has long been the graveyard for armoured vehicles. It has seen the Iran-Iraq war, the Gulf War, the Iraq conflict as well as civil war in Yemen. Since the creation of Israel in 1948 – the temperature of Arab -Israeli relations has regularly soared. Israeli tank units have fought a number of conflicts with various Arab forces, most notably in 1948–49, then in 1956, the six-day war in 1967, the Yom Kippur fight in 1973, the war in Lebanon 1982 and 2006 as well as the current conflict in Gaza. In 1969 the Israel Defense Forces announced that Tel Aviv's home built, and developed tank had entered service - the Merkava. It has remained in frontline operational service since its first deployment in the Lebanon War in 1982, where it performed well against Soviet-era

RIGHT: At one time the Soviet-era T-72 was dominant in the Middle East but today Western tanks have increased their footprint. US DoD

BELOW: The Middle East has long been the graveyard of armoured vehicles. Yves DeBay/DPL

RIGHT: A disabled Israeli Centurion during the Yom Kipper war. IDF

T-72 tanks used by the Syrian Army in the Beqaa Valley.

The decision to build an indigenous tank began in 1974, after the Yom Kippur war, in which Tel Aviv's armoured forces had suffered heavy losses among their American M60 and British Centurion tanks. Israel had suffered problems purchasing new tanks after a planned procurement from the UK fell through. During the 1960s Britain had sold more than 200 Centurions to Israel and had begun a joint-venture with Tel Aviv for a new tank, the Chieftain. The aim being that Tel Aviv would procure the tank and domestically manufacture the vehicle. A four-year study included the delivery of two prototypes, but ultimately the UK decided not to move ahead with the project amid concerns that it would impact on the UK's relationship with Arab nations across the Middle East. Israel therefore decided to end its reliance on foreign aid and instead design and develop its own tank. »

New Capability

The latest incarnation of the Merkava, the Barak, is fitted with a digital capability that takes data from tracked units and unmanned aerial vehicles operating with the Merkavas. The system displays the information on colour screens and distributes it in encrypted form to all other units in a given area. The tank has a high-performance air conditioning system and can be fitted with a toilet for long-duration missions. In July 2018 as part of the plans for the new Barak variant the integration of the Iron Vision helmet mounted augmented reality system was introduced. This incorporated the use high-resolution cameras arrayed around the tank to provide a 360° view of a tank's surroundings to helmet displays worn by crew members. These upgrades were fielded in 2023 as the IDF rolled out the Barak. It has an enhancement to the Trophy APS as well as new light sensitive, 360° day/night camera coverage for boosted situational awareness. The cameras being housed in blast proof boxes. The tank commander wears a fighter jet–style helmet enabling him or her to independently acquire targets and direct strikes rapidly. The tank also has an electronic warfare capability and advanced processing systems to intercept communications and close-down civilian internet systems. A direct energy system capable of intercepting drones and cruise missiles is also installed. The Merkava Mark IV tank also has enhanced armour on top of the turret, providing more protection to the crew against drone strikes.

At the heart of this new technology the secret Trophy ASPS system allegedly relies heavily on high-speed computational technologies. On detection of an incoming projectile, the system automatically computes various parameters, such as the approach vector, nature of the threat, time to impact, and angle of approach. The defensive projectiles are launched by two rotating launchers positioned on the sides of the vehicle. These launchers deploy a number of small EFPs (Explosive Formed Penetrators) and present an immediate block to the incoming projectile. The system has been engineered with a narrow kill zone to ensure the safety of friendly personnel in close proximity to the protected vehicle. Trophy is a system that enables connectivity to other technologies, such as 'soft kill' remote command and control systems that direct weapon systems. The system is designed to defend against many types of anti-tank guided missiles, rockets, and high explosive rounds. It can simultaneously engage numerous threats arriving from different directions and is said to be effective while stationary or moving. Newer versions of the system include an automated reloading feature for multiple firings of defensive counter measures. »

BELOW: An Israeli Merkava Barak fitted with Trophy armoured protection. IDF

ABOVE: A Merkava Barak moving at speed, these tanks are among the most protected in the world. IDF

RIGHT: The Barak, the latest generation Merkava tank in service. IDF

THE MERKAVA

ABOVE: In service since 2004, the Merkava Mk IV features a powerful 120mm main gun and modular armour that can be replaced relatively quickly if damaged.
Tank Encyclopedia

RIGHT: Israel's Merkava tank pictured during the Lebanon war. IDF

BELOW: An Israeli Merkava crew, the rear door in the tank can clearly be seen in the centre of the vehicle. IDF

The Merkava, 'chariot' in Hebrew, is a revolutionary tank whose development was pioneered by General Israel Tal as a result of lessons learned in the Yom Kippur war. Packed with technology and sensors designed to give the crew greater situational awareness, this is a tank which no other country has had access to through exports or exchange. This unique tank, with its engine at the front for better crew protection is continually being evolved. Since the introduction of the first variant the armour has been significantly advanced.

All variants of the Merkava incorporate a unique capability that allows them to operate as makeshift armoured personnel carriers or ambulances. This is achieved by taking out the palleted ammunition racks in the rear of the tank which provides space for ten soldiers or walking wounded to be transported – entering through the rear door. While this function has been rehearsed on manoeuvres, it is not believed to have been used on operations until the current conflict in Gaza in which Merkavas have been used to evacuate wounded soldiers.

In September 2023 the Israel Defense Forces revealed the latest variant of the Merkava, called the Mark IV Barak. From the outside the tank looks like any other Merkava but this is a 'smart tank' which has the ability to fight drones and counter anti-tank missiles before they can contact the tank's armour. Its low profile, 120mm main armament and top-secret armour have shaped the Merkava as a chariot of war. Since entering service, the tank has undergone numerous upgrades to a design that incorporates 'smart technology' with cameras and artificial intelligence added to the platform. Each generation of the tank has increased survivability and the Merkava IV fielded a new Trophy anti-tank missile shield when it began production in 2004. The Trophy system provides 360° protection for

MERKAVA MAIN BATTLE TANK SPECIFICATION

Model	MERKAVA
Manufacturer	Mantank IDF Ordnance Corps
Country	Israel
Year	1979
Engine	MTU 12V 883 - 1119 kW (1,501hp) turbo -charged diesel
Fuel	Diesel
Protection	7039 aluminium alloy hulls, Rolled Homogeneous Steel turret
Top Speed	40mph on a surfaced road
Range	310 miles
Crew Capacity	Four – commander, driver, gunner, loader.
Length	29ft
Width	12ft
Height	8ft
Armament	120mm (4.7in) smoothbore gun, capable of firing LAHAT and ATGM
Weight	65 tonnes
Service Branch	Israel Defense Forces

RIGHT: A Merkava tank in south Lebanon during the war. IDF

RIGHT: A Merkava tank on the Lebanon-Syrian border during the war. IDF

BELOW: A Merkava firing a fully loaded live charge. IDF

plaudits during the Lebanon war and quickly gained a reputation as a significant success. It outperformed contemporary Syrian T-62 tanks and proved to have strong resistance against anti-tank weapons such as the AT-3 Sager and the RPG-7. The tank was a major improvement over Israel's previous Centurion main battle tank. The turret design has an unusual, angled shape designed to deflect projectiles.

the tank and can intercept multiple incoming anti-tank missiles. In 2023 the fifth generation of the tank entered service. The IDF have revealed that the upgrades include the Iron Vision smart helmet – which delivers the same concept as Israel's 'Iron Dome' anti-missile system. Sensors on the outside of the tank allow the commander to see outside the tank with peripheral vision that is knitted together from sensors and cameras which feed into the vehicle's protection system to intercept and destroy any threat.

Unlike Soviet-era tanks the Merkava was designed to protect the crew. The unusual decision to place the engine at the front was questioned by many. It allowed the crew to enter and exit from behind, even under fire. The tank was adapted for desert terrain, particularly specialising in long-range fire. The Merkava had gained

At the time of its introduction to the battlefield the Merkava Mk.1 was one of the most protected tanks in the world. The Mark 1 weighed 63 tonnes and had a 908-horsepower diesel engine. It was armed with the 105mm main gun and two 7.62mm machine guns. In addition, it had a 60mm mortar mounted externally. The tracks and road wheels copied the British Centurion tank, and the 105mm was made under license from the US.

Although the tanks were a success, the M113 armoured personnel carriers that accompanied the Merkavas suffered a number of problems, both mechanical and as a result of enemy fire. Consequently, the Merkavas underwent the previously mentioned modification that allows the palleted ammunition racks to be removed to create capacity for ten soldiers or walking wounded. Regular adjustments and additions have been noted and built in, including the need for the 60mm mortar to be installed within the hull and engineered for remote firing. Heavy chain netting was also fitted to the gap between the hull and turret at the rear to ensure that rocket propelled grenades ignited before they hit the tank.

UKRAINE'S TANKS

Involved in a war since invasion by Russia two years ago, Ukraine has long been the key player in Eastern Europe's tank development.

Ukraine's Armour

Ukraine has long been an economic powerhouse of eastern Europe with steelworks across the region producing the raw material for industry to manufacture everything from buses to battlefield tanks. The most notable of these is the T-64, produced in the early 1960s and deployed to eastern Germany with Soviet troops. Prior to the Russian invasion in 2022, Kyiv forces had more than 900 tanks in service – many of them homemade.

A significant number were old and inherited when the Soviet Union collapsed in 1991. Ukraine inherited eight Guards tank regiments which were based in the country, and which quickly boosted its armoured strength.

The T-64 tank is the most common tank Ukraine has today. It was more advanced than the T-62 with heavier armour and the main gun was replaced with new smoothbore 125mm gun. It also introduced a number of advanced features

including composite armour, a new compact engine and transmission, the gun was also equipped with an autoloader to allow the crew to be reduced to three so the tank could be smaller and lighter. The T-64 weighs just 38 tonnes and with its 700-horsepower diesel engine was a very powerful vehicle. These features made the T-64 expensive to build, significantly more so than previous generations of Soviet tanks. This was especially true of the powerplant, which was time-consuming to

ABOVE: A Ukrainian T-64 during the 2021 liberation parade in Kyiv.
Voider Wander

LEFT: A T-64 made in Ukraine which was deployed in East Germany during the Cold War. US DoD

build and cost twice as much as more conventional designs. Several proposals were made to improve the T-64 with new cheaper engines but the design was maintained in production in spite of any concerns about cost. The result was a fast,

heavily-armed, and armoured tank that, on paper at least matched contemporary Western tanks.

From 1991 the Ukrainian ground forces continued to buy its military equipment from Russia and continued to produce hardware

for Moscow. Ukraine's Kharkov Morozov Machine Building Design Bureau had designed armoured vehicles in the 1970s including the T-80D and the T-84UD as well as T-84 main battle tanks – which entered service in 1999. However, »

BELOW: A T-64 Bulat variant taking part in Ukraine's liberation day parade. Voider Wander

LEFT: A Ukrainian T-72 which has been modernised during the war.
Ukraine MoD

following Russia's annexation of Crimea in 2014 and support for separatist forces in eastern Ukraine, fighting erupted in the east for almost eight years in what Kyiv called the 'forgotten war'. Ukraine sought NATO membership, formally declaring it a strategic policy objective in 2017, and Western forces deployed training teams and instructed Ukrainian forces how to fight, particularly against tanks. Key in their training was to avoid the Warsaw Pact approach, which they had been trained in, of attacking from the front, a key element of classic Soviet armoured and infantry doctrine. By late 2021 Ukraine had more than 500 tanks ready for operations and a new mindset about how to deploy them.

Russian Invasion

On February 22, 2022, more than 1,700 Russian T-72 tanks moved across the border with the aim of seizing Kyiv. With their newly learnt anti-tank skills the Ukrainians were able to attack and disable the Russian tank columns, in one incident destroying an entire convoy, while President Zelensky ordered his armoured units to advance and take on the Russians. Kyiv sent forward regiments of tanks and attacked from the flank, laid traps for the Russians, and used deception operations to hoodwink them. By December 2022, Ukraine had captured 308 Russian

T-72 tanks - a number which was boosted with 260 T-72s from Poland. Despite the new, additional armour, Ukraine's tanks were quickly outnumbered by Moscow's forces and Zelensky appealed to the West for help.

On January 11, 2023, the United Kingdom announced plans to send modern heavy tanks to Ukraine and donated 14 Challengers which were delivered to Ukraine along with a large number of Leopard tanks. A German-Danish-Dutch

BELOW: Ukrainian tanks and infantry attacked a Russian armoured column in Bucha – destroying the entire convoy.
Ukraine MoD

consortium initially announced it would donate to Ukraine's war effort an initial batch of 100 German-made Leopard 1A5 tanks. Denmark pledged another 95 with Germany stating it would increase its number. By November 2023, the first 20 or so Leopard 1A5s had already arrived in Ukraine, where they equipped a company within the new 44th Mechanized Brigade. Spain and Poland later donated Leopard 2s, while the Czech Republic donated more than 70 T-72s. The United

States stated they would donate 31 M1 Abrams tanks to Ukraine, and they arrived in late 2023.

Ukraine's tank army of T-64s also included hundreds of fake 'inflatable' tanks which were used to draw Putin's armour into ambushes. By early 2024 intelligence analysts reported that an American Abrams tank had been destroyed and another captured – it was taken to Moscow and put on display. In the same week two Leopards and a Challenger were reported to have been destroyed, although details of how they were lost are unclear.

Drones quickly became a threat to Russian T-72s. They were armed with explosives, shaped charges, and in some case just grenades. In a response the Russians quickly welded

metal shields to the top of the tanks to protect them from drone and N-Law attacks – these have become known as cope cages. They protect against some but not all top-attack weapons. While they offer some protection against Excalibur rounds and some similar older artillery munitions, the cages cannot protect against Javelin anti-tank missiles as the Javelin missile has a direct attack mode which may circumvent the cage. Finally, the protection against N-LAW is limited as in direct attack mode it rises as it approaches the target and has a 45° attack angle when striking the turret. As of April 2024, analysts stated that more than 2,900 Russian tanks have been lost in Ukraine – 1,432 of them T-72s. Kyiv has also fielded »

ABOVE: A Ukrainian anti-tank team seconds after attacking a Russian T-72.
Ukraine MoD

BELOW: A Destroyed Russian T-72 tank which appears to have its armoured shield still intact.
Ukraine MoD

ABOVE: Russian tank crews are now building metal sheds around their vehicles to protect against aerial attacks and Ukrainian tanks.
Ukraine MoD

(ERA) appeared. It had clearly been hit by a tank shell or missile and its ammunition 'cooked 'off' but the Kontakt blocks appeared to have survived.

The high casualty rate among the Russian T-72s has a lot to do with their lack of technology – many of Moscow's tanks have no system to warn, track and counter threats such as N-LAW missiles, many are old, and reliability has also been a major issue. While Western tanks have tended to store their ammunition in the back of the turret, away from the crew, the ammunition in the T-72 sits directly beneath the turret and the crew and the results can be catastrophic if the tank is hit. Additionally, the Russian logistic supply train to get ammunition and spare parts to the T-72s in the frontline appears to have been compromised many times. The number of T-72s that have sunk while crossing rivers suggests that crews were unfamiliar with wading drills or did not have the necessary equipment. In April 2024, a T-72 operating in the Donetsk region hit an obstacle and was disabled. Ukraine immediately hit the sitting duck target with an armed drone. Its three-person crew were killed as they baled out, but the tank sustained only minimal damage and Kyiv wanted to capture it. It had a bizarre mass of antennae and transmitters strapped to its turret. The improvised electronic warfare system that looked like it might be trying to block radio signals between the attack drones and their operators. But the jammer hadn't worked, and

Ukraine needed to know why. The fearsome 12th Azov Brigade found the tank, replaced its batteries, and started it up. Then, the T-72 had to be driven across bomb-blitzed terrain to Ukraine while being shot at by Russian artillery. What they found wasn't a fearsome new jamming weapon, but a taped-together mismatched jumble of antennae and transmitters. Russia has faced criticism of its electronic warfare systems - often badly-made and badly-assembled - but this incident appeared to be a deception.

In the past 18 months Ukrainian tanks have operated in conjunction with infantry, anti-tank teams , artillery, and drone units – a clear adoption of the 'combined arms policy' to integrate frontline forces. This has resulted in Kyiv's forces being able to identify targets and attack them by artillery or tanks while deploying N-LAW manned units to ambush tanks with the smart anti-tank missile. Such is their success that Russian tanks have built 'metal sheds' around their T-72s.

Open-source reporting highlights that tank losses in Ukraine are compelling and that despite having fewer tanks than the invaders, the Ukrainian army appears to have used theirs well. Their success has forced the Russian army to retrofit even older T-62 tanks for combat service. With the introduction of Challenger 2s, Leopard 1s, Leopard 2s, and M1A1 Abrams into Ukrainian service, Russian tank crews have been under orders to 'kill' Western tanks any cost – with reports that commanders have offered financial

T-72s, which mainly included T-72As and T-72AVs, as well as modernised T-72AMTs. This force was boosted with the captured Russian T-72s which Ukraine repaired and used against the invaders. It was believed that the Russian tanks were fitted with Kontakt armour and on April 3, 2022, an image of a rare T-72 'Ural' of 1973 vintage, equipped with Kontakt-1 explosive reactive armour

RIGHT: A German Leopard tank in Ukraine – more than 200 are reported to be in service with Kyiv's forces. Ukraine MoD

LEFT: A Ukrainian tank crew member pictured inside a Leopard tank during operations in Ukraine.
Ukraine MoD

rewards for those who are successful. Technology alone is not the key to modern armoured warfare. As World War Two demonstrated, tactics are fundamental to success. The Russian and Ukrainian armies are branches of the same tree, inheritors of the same Soviet Red Army training. As such, their common doctrine for tank warfare was shaped by the pioneering tactics of Marshal Georgy Konstantinovich Zhukov. Zhukov's doctrine which employed tank forces as a mobile sledgehammer – with a philosophy of 'stacks of smoke and straight up the middle- meaning a direct frontal attack. However, Zhukov died in 1974 and his philosophy may be being trumped by more modern, flexible thinking.

Ukrainian tank crews were given training in the UK, but it would have been challenging to absorb a completely different tactical approach in the six-week package as well as learning how to operate the Leopard, Abrams, and Challenger. The Western approach is grounded in a cavalry-based philosophy – move fast, strike hard. However, the apparent success of the Ukrainian forces would seem to indicate that the lessons were indeed learned and are proving effective.

Built in Ukraine

For generations, Ukraine built Soviet tanks at its factories in Kharkiv where skilled workers delivered main battle tanks on a regular basis. That was prior to the Russian invasion, and since February 2022 Moscow's

firepower has destroyed both factories and machinery. The premier tank made here was the T-72. From Ukraine, tanks went to Iraq, Libya, and across the Middle East. In Surrey, Ivan, a former manager at one of the factories is now in the UK on

a military training course to prepare him for combat. In his 50s, Ivan said most of the factory where he worked had been destroyed. He said: "These were good tanks, powered by a V-46 diesel engine, our workers were skilled and very good, and we had ❯❯

BELOW: Ukrainian troops captured a Russian tank they thought was fitted with electronic counter measures.
Ukraine MoD

LEFT: A Ukrainian T-64 during the winter months of the Ukraine war. Kyryl Savin

an excellent reputation, our tanks went everywhere".

The T-72 is configured with six large roadwheels similar to those on the T-55 and T-62 series tanks. The tank also boasts a self-entrenching blade and can dig trenches within 40 minutes, or as quickly as 12 minutes for certain 'soft' ground types. With a maximum speed of 37mph, the operational range of the tank is 290 miles increasing to 430 miles with fuel drums, which are carried at the rear. The tank is also capable of crossing rivers up to 16ft deep submerged using a small diameter snorkel. The crew is individually supplied with rebreather chest packs for emergency situations. Crews regularly rehearsed drills in-case of accidents which were some of the least popular training events. If the engine stops underwater, it must be restarted within six seconds, or the T-72's engine compartment becomes flooded due to pressure loss. The snorkelling procedure is considered dangerous but is important for

maintaining operational mobility. The T-72 has a nuclear, biological, and chemical (NBC) protection system. The inside of both hull and turret is lined with a synthetic fabric, meant to reduce the penetrating radiation from a nuclear explosion. The crew is supplied clean air via an air filter system. A slight over-pressure prevents entry of contamination.

Use of an autoloader for the main gun allows for more efficient forced smoke removal compared to traditional manually loaded tank guns, so NBC isolation of the fighting compartment can, in theory, be maintained indefinitely. A radiation detector is located on the right hand of the turret compartment and is designed to monitor any pollution that could impact the crew. Because the T-72 lacked space inside the turret there is little room to add recent technology, such as integrated battlefield systems which shows the disposition of friendly forces and enemy tanks or camera screens to enhance the driver's visibility

through chassis mounted cameras. The tank was regarded by many as a tank for its time in the 1970s and 80s, but unable to complete with modern platforms such as Abrams, Leopard, and Challenger.

Armour protection on the T-72 has been strengthened with each succeeding generation. The original T-72 'Ural' Object 172M's (from 1973) turret is made from conventional cast, high hardness, steel (HHS) armour with no laminate inserts. It is believed that the maximum thickness is 11in and the nose is 3.1in. The glacis of the new laminated armour is 205mm (8.1in) thick, including 3.1in of HHS. An upgrade of the tank, the T-72A featured a new turret with a thicker, nearly vertical, frontal. This included new ceramic-rod turret filler, incorporated improved glacis laminate armour, and mounted new anti-shaped-charge side skirts. Further protection came with the introduction of explosive reactive armour (ERA).

BELOW: Ukrainian T-64 tanks in the early months of the Russian invasion. Kyryl Savin

Due to the visible bulging shape of the 'up-armoured' turret front it was nicknamed 'Dolly Parton' armour by US tank crews. However, much of the additional armour was not available on export models. Following the collapse of the USSR, US and German analysts had a chance to examine Soviet-made T-72 tanks equipped with ERA, and they proved impenetrable to most Cold War US and German tank projectiles and anti-tank weapons. In the 1982 war in Lebanon a number of Syrian T-72s were destroyed by Israeli tanks and anti-tank missile units. This suggested that while the tank was fit for purpose in the 1970s, the export models had not received armour upgrades. In addition, many T-72 s sold to Arab states did not include the complex integrated fire control system which had been replaced with a more traditional range finder. Under licence, the T-72 was produced in Poland, India, and Czechoslovakia. The variant had side skirts to protect the running wheels, as well as smoke grenade launchers, an enlarged view finder and external stowage for additional machine gun ammunition. However, snorkel equipment fitted to the side of the turret prevented some of the storage boxes from being opened!

Export

The T-72 had been procured by countries across the globe and it is estimated that 20,000 of the type are still in service. It is estimated more than 30,000 T-72 tanks were built,

making it one of the most widely produced post-World War Two tanks, second only to the T-54/55 family. The T-72A version introduced in 1979 is considered a second-generation main battle tank. It saw service in 40 countries and in numerous conflicts. One of the biggest sales was to Iraq. At the end of the 1990s, Russia operated an estimated 9,000 T-72s main battle tanks and sold hundreds of variants to Baghdad which they used in their invasion of Kuwait. But the imported tanks had little technology and lacked laser range finders, night visions and good communications. In 2003 a small number of T-72s manned by the Saddam's Republican Guard fought well, but most of the Iraqi tanks were quickly destroyed by advancing US Abrams and British Challenger tanks.

The T-72 was a major export success and was used by Algeria, Bulgaria, Belarus, Georgia, Hungary, Iran, India, Kenya, Libya, Malaya, Morocco, Nigeria, Finland, Yugoslavia, East Germany, Yemen, The Democratic Republic of the Congo, and Ukraine. The T-72 has been used in combat more than any other tank. It was first deployed in the Iran-Iraq war in 1980, it was then used by Syria in the 1982 Lebanon conflict. Later, Ethiopia used the tank in their dispute with Somalia. In the Sri Lankan civil war, the First Nagarro – Karabakh war in 1984, in Georgia, the Gulf war, in Sierra Leone, the Yugoslav wars, Kosovo and Macedonia. By 2000 the T-72 was still in the frontline in Algeria, Iraq, Tajikistan, Rwanda, the Chechen war, and the Sudan war. »

LEFT: A Ukrainian T-72 pictured during the first few months of the conflict. Ukraine MoD

LEFT: A T-72 pictured in a wood line east of Kyiv just weeks after the Russia invasion. Ukraine MoD

BELOW: A Ukrainian T-72 crew member – bullet holes from a heavy calibre weapon can be seen on the tanks armour. Ukraine MoD

THE T-72

The Soviet T-72 entered service in the early 1970s and has become a core asset of Ukraine's forces. The tank is one of the remarkable success stories of armoured history. The tank is fast, dependable, and cost-effective. Work started back in the 1950s, when Soviet tank manufacturers were directed to develop a platform to replace the obsolete T-54 and T-55. Such work was conducted in two design bureaus, one of them the Design Bureau in Kharkiv – where the successful T-64, was designed - and a factory in Nizhny Tagil was also invited to rework the T-64. It had already prepared a main battle tank design, which had a new chassis, new engine, the introduction of an autoloader with 115mm and 125mm main gun options. The resulting tank was codenamed Object 172 and was fitted with an engine made in Nizhny Tagil, while the T-64 chassis was still used. The new engine made the tank heavier by 1.5 tons.

After several upgrades, the Object 172 received a refurbished chassis, which together with the autoloader and other equipment was also designed by Uralvagonzavod (UVZ). It was actually a new tank compared with the original. Uralvagonzavod's designers were also able to solve a critical task for production of a main battle tank for a large army – to make a cheaper and simpler vehicle compared with its predecessor, while maintaining all combat capabilities. After all tests, the new T-72 'Ural' entered service with the Soviet Army on August 7, 1973. The new 'Ural' benefitted from low clearance, good speed, strong protection, and high armament capability. An upgraded T-72A was fielded and mastered for mass production in 1979, a powerful T-72B was fielded in 1984, and since then a wide number of upgrades have been fielded.

The striking characteristic of the T-72 was its low profile – smaller than any NATO tanks of the time - which was aimed at giving it a tactical advantage on the battlefield. This had been achieved by careful design and at the expense of the loader's position – which was replaced with technology – an automatic loading carousel. This was revolutionary as it delivered a constant feed of ammunition to the gun and was based on the system used in the BMP armoured personnel carrier. The commander selected the ammunition, and the projectile was hoisted onto the circular loading system. The gunner then lifts the cassette, and the round is loaded into the breech.

T-72 – MAIN BATTLE TANK (NUMEROUS VARIANTS) SPECIFICATION

Model	T-72 MBT
Manufacturer	Design Bureau in Kharkiv (Ukraine) | Nizhny Tagil (Russia)
Country	Ukraine and Russia
Year	1989–90
Engine	V-12 diesel 780hp
Fuel	Diesel
Protection	Steel and composite armour with ERA
Top Speed	40mph (64kph)
Range	290 miles (466km), extends to 430 miles with external fuel drums (692km)
Crew Capacity	Crew of three
Length	31ft
Width	12ft
Height	7ft
Armament	125mm 2A46M/2A46M-5 smoothbore gun, support from 12.7mm heavy machine gun
Weight	41 tonnes
Service Branch	Ukraine | Russia

On completion the spent round is automatically ejected. The autoloader supported a maximum rate of fire of up to eight rounds per minute. This was a major improvement on the one or two rounds per minute when loaded manually and gave the T-72 a further edge when first introduced. But the initial autoloader was often reported as being unreliable and resulted in manual loading by the gunner, which was slow and difficult. An upgrade resolved the issue.

When fully loaded the tank carried 39 rounds with an effective shooting range of 2,000-3,000m in the daylight and 850-1,300m at night. While the loader's job had been axed, little space was given to the crew in what must be one of the most confined and claustrophobic spaces inside a tank since the early platforms of World War One. Soviet tanks were so cramped that height constraints were put in place for the crew, with a maximum height of 5ft 4in – this was due to the small leg room for

the commander and gunner. Official regulations stated a height of 5 ft 9in for tank crews - which was standard for other tanks at the time. The basic T-72 design has extremely limited and in 2024 Ukrainian crews still complain about the lack of room.

ABOVE LEFT: A Ukrainian T-72A with an improvised mine clearing system fitted to the front. Ukraine MoD

LEFT: The T-72 is still regarded as one of the best tanks of all time. US DoD

BELOW: A T-72 crew take a break in the winter weather. US DoD

RUSSIA AND THE FUTURE

The battlefield is constantly changing. Tank design, anti-tank tactics and technology have to keep pace with that change.

Changing Batttlefield

In the 21st century, tank warfare, or mechanised battle, is changing as threats evolve and the demand for greater firepower and protection increases. Future tank warfare will see platforms fitted with systems that deliver enhanced situational awareness, artificial intelligence will be factored into computers to analyse algorithms that help identify targets and counter incoming missiles. In the past decade the quest for improved crew protection has resulted in tanks getting heavier. Big tanks require bigger engines, more fuel, and extended logistics which increases the cost of development and risks expanding the 'weight waistline' of the modern tank. Weight feeds into operational delivery: a C-17 transport plane can carry 68 tonnes and the projected weight of the future AbramsX and the Challenger 3 are both listed to be in excess of 65 tonnes. Scientists are working towards developing lightweight armour that has the properties of systems such as enhanced Chobham. Their aim is to produce a super light composite that could potentially also be used to protect helicopters and even warships operating in contested waters. Lighter, but still protected tanks will mean that armour can be flown forward in transport aircraft

RIGHT: Britain is one of several nations looking to upgrade the tank they have in service. MoD

and ferried ashore - avoiding the top heavy 65 tonnes plus weight that many modern tanks are heading for with traditional armour upgrades. The Israeli's latest generation Merkava, the Barak, has set the standard in armoured firepower and protection for future warfare, but at a huge cost – the Barak weighs 65 tonnes.

The open countryside is best suited to tank warfare, but events in both Ukraine and Gaza have shown that increasingly, modern operations will involve the urban environments where tanks can be trapped and disabled. The Russian war in Chechnya in 1994 was an example of how vulnerable armour can be. Moscow sent tanks into Grozny, expecting a quick victory. However, Chechen units had organised into combat groups, typically composed of around 20 personnel, further divided into three- or four-person fire teams. Each fire team consisted of an anti-tank gunner armed with Russian-made RPG-7 or RPG-18 and a machine gunner. To effectively engage Russian armoured vehicles in Grozny, multiple fire teams coordinated their actions on the ground level, as well as in second

and third-storey positions and basements. Snipers and machine gunners provided suppressive fire on the supporting infantry, while the anti-tank gunners engaged any armoured vehicles.

The War on Terror changed the military view of the tank,

in Afghanistan the threat was primarily from insurgents and while the invasion of Iraq was a major armoured operation, in the main, with the notable exception of some Republican Guard units, the Iraqi army did not stand and fight. Senior US commanders battled for »

ABOVE: The United States has explored developing an 'extra size' Abrams called the AbramsX. US DoD

CHALLENGER 3

In May 2024, the British Army successfully conducted firing tests in Germany, highlighting the exceptional long-range capabilities of the new Challenger 3 main battle tank (MBT). Central to these tests was the tank's cutting-edge 120mm Rheinmetall L55A1 high-pressure gun, paired with the latest 120mm DM73 ammunition, enabling a range of engagement of up to 5,000m. At the heart of the Challenger 3's main armament, this new smoothbore gun is a notable improvement over the rifled gun used in the Challenger 2, marking a shift to smoothbore technology which is more compatible with modern NATO ammunition standards.

The L55A1 is an extended version of the earlier L44 gun, featuring a barrel length of 55 calibres (approximately 6.6m). This longer barrel enhances the muzzle velocity of projectiles, contributing to greater accuracy and penetrating power.

LEFT: Germany has developed a totally new, futuristic looking main battle tank. Rheinmetall

BELOW: The new German tank is being considered in a joint venture with France. Rheinmetall

ABOVE: Tanks are getting bigger and risk being too large to fly. Rheinmetall

RIGHT: The French Leclerc is due to be replaced and Paris has joined a tank venture with Berlin. French MoD

RIGHT: The future Abrams, if the US opt to go ahead with it, could weigh almost 68 tonnes. US DoD

revenue to be invested in dismounted forces while others called for additional funding for new tanks.

The view of many commanders is that modern weapons are challenging the role of the tank and in some cases insurgents who have the freedom of movement are shaping the future of tank warfare. Israel's use of speed, surprise, and firepower worked well in the first few days of the war in Gaza but once tanks entered towns the situation changed. Progress is slow as the tank's sensors search for threats from mines and IEDs. In many cases the tanks are forced to take up stationary positions, to provide overwatch to troops – leaving them vulnerable to attack.

Today tanks are to be found in proxy wars, asymmetric warfare as well as full scale war-fighting. In the Yemen, Iranian backed Houthi rebels used captured Saudi tanks against government forces in Aden. IEDs and roadside bombs are feared by armoured forces and in Syria insurgents used roadside bombs to shape the battlefield by seeding devices on key supply routes and forcing government tanks to take an alternative routes – which the terrorists attacked at a time of their choosing

In Ukraine, total war has seen tank-on-tank conflict. Commanders are well aware that an infantry force armed with guided missile launchers can devastate tank units. It happened when large numbers of Israeli tanks were attacked by the Egyptian Malyutka anti-tank guided missile squad during the 1973 Yom Kippur War. And in 1986, Libyan tanks were hit hard in the so called 'Toyota War' with Chad.

ABOVE: Even modern tanks like the Merkava have been forced to add basic cope cages to protect from drone attacks. IDF

RIGHT: The Israeli Merkava is said to be one of the most advanced tanks in the world. IDF

Drones are the new weapon of the 21st century, cheap, easy to operate and highly effective. While the war in Ukraine has seen the exploitation of the unmanned aerial vehicles (UAV) they had first deployed with devastating effect when Azerbaijan used loitering munitions against Armenian tanks – mostly Soviet era platforms. The manoeuvre of tanks is vital if they are to deliver their capability. Swarming drones and loitering munitions are getting 'smarter' and many tank technologies are not keeping up with them. Many scientists see future tank designs incorporating their own drone system which can be deployed to both fight an enemy and attack enemy drones. Experts see the ability to control the electronic frequency

of a drone as the ultimate way to counter unmanned platforms. Currently, drone teams can overlay a 'ghost' frequency and electronically hide their platforms, leaving both Ukrainian and Russian forces having to resort to shooting down drones.

Armata's Armour

In 2014, Russia announced that it had developed the most advanced tank in the world – the T-14 Armata. And when it first appeared in public in 2015 it certainly impressed, was packed with capability and stunned many Western military commanders. It was the first new Russian tank development since the end of the Cold War and was a step change away from the adopted Western practice of upgrading tanks in service.

The Armata's armour remains one of the Kremlin's closely guarded secrets. It has been reported that a new Malachite Explosive Reactive Armour (ERA), has been fitted to the T-14 which is designed to counteract impacting projectiles with an explosive force away from the tank. Again, it is unclear how this process is activated without a threat to the tank itself. The T-14's design has considered future unconventional asymmetric threats and has the capability to add modular applique armour fixed to the side skirts in respect of the operational threat. The addition of armour imposes a significant weight problem to the performance of the engine and transmission. Unconfirmed reports have suggested the Russians have developed a new ballistic lightweight armour which has the characteristics of the active protection system (APS) but does not carry the weight penalty. The T-14 is known to have been fitted with the Afganit APS - this hi-tech system uses radar and electro-optical sensors in what are described as 'in the ultraviolet and infrared bands'. The millimetre-wavelength radar then detects and tracks incoming anti-tank munitions and activates weapon capabilities to counter the attack. The system can reportedly intercept armour piercing, fin stabilised discarding sabot kinetic energy penetrators – used by NATO forces- as well as high explosive anti-tank (HEAT) rounds. If true, this is a significant concern for Western alliance forces. In addition, the system protects the tank from all sides, enhancing the combat »

effectiveness. However, many analysts have questioned why this alleged new capability has yet to be deployed in Ukraine.

The protection levels and projected firepower of the T-14 are significant, but its success on the battlefield will be determined by the crew's ability to utilise these new capabilities to best effect, within a tactical formation, often called a combined arms group. Advanced sights, sensors and fire-control systems are no doubt employed; the APS may also have an important situational awareness role. Its tracking of incoming threats may also enable its use as a counter-fire radar, as per the Trophy system, enabling accurate return fire and potentially providing enemy locations to other nearby friendly forces.

The Armata currently mounts a 125mm smoothbore cannon, but

RIGHT: The driver and commander of an Armata appear to have an enhance vision through multiple periscopes.
Russian MoD

ABOVE: Unlike the German Leopard and other European tanks, the Russian Armata has a flat glacis at the front of the tank.
Russian MoD

observers suggest the turret ring and size of the T-14 will support Moscow's' planned intention to upgrade to 152mm, which would be the largest calibre gun ever mounted on an operational post-war MBT. The precise armour-penetrating properties of a 152mm main gun are unclear, but the sheer kinetic energy increase associated with this larger calibre weapon will deliver a major challenge to even the latest Western armour. In addition, Russia also claims the current 125mm cannon will be able to fire new anti-tank guided missiles (ATGMs).

Crew stations are also highly digitised in terms of interface and control providing multiple information feeds on crew screens. Having removed the crew from the turret, the T-14's manufacturer, Uralvagonzavod, also envisions a

potential future unmanned ground vehicle variant which will operate ahead of the T-14 with one obvious role being mine clearing.

The development of the T-14 was shrouded in secrecy, like all Russian military projects. It emerged after the cancellation of Russia's T-95 project which was a casualty of the troubled 1990s and was finally abandoned in 2010 when a design study began for the Armata. It resulted in the Object 148 programme based on the T-95.

The T-14 first publicly appeared in March 2015, when several tanks with covered turrets were seen loaded on train carriages in Alabino. Later one was seen on May 9, 2015 during the rehearsal for the Moscow Victory Parade when one of the tanks broke down, requiring maintenance before it could move off again. Seven T-14 Armata tanks appeared in the 2015 and 2016 parades and again in 2017 and 2018. The official military trials of the tank started in early 2020 when the then Minister of Industry and Trade Denis Manturov announced that the new T-14 had already been evaluated in combat conditions in Syria. Exactly how the T-14 performed in Syria has not been revealed, but many experts in the area of armoured vehicles suggest that the T-14's engine is the Achilles heel of the tank. Previous Russian tanks – with the exception of the T-64 - have used variants of the highly successful V-2 diesel engine designed in 1931 at Kharkov Locomotive Plant in Ukraine which has since been destroyed in Russia's war. A series of improved V-2 engines

At the same time new 'traditional' anti-tank systems are forcing change, particularly after lessons learned in Ukraine. The NLAW anti-tank missile destroyed dozens of Russian tanks with its 'smart technology'. The operator can simply aim at the visible part and fire. The missile will travel one metre above the line of sight before it takes the tank out from above. From the time the trigger is pressed the NLAW takes six seconds to hunt, lock-on, and destroy a target. Tanks have traditionally allowed their operators to hunt opponents in relative safety. NLAW turns the tables by removing this safety level, earning its name as the ultimate tank killer. Extremely flexible, NLAW can attack from almost any position, from up high in a building to behind a tree or in a ditch. You can fire down 45° and can shoot from inside a building, from a basement or from the second floor of a building out of the range of most tanks. »

LEFT: The underside of the Armata is heavily armoured to protect from mines. Russian MoD

BELOW: This image shows a new package of armour which can be added pending the operation. Russian MoD

BOTTOM: Sensors on the turret of the Armata seem potentially exposed to damage in conflict. Russian MoD

were used in the T-72, the BMP series of armoured personnel carriers and the T-90. The V-2 is highly regarded as unbreakable and viewed as the Kalashnikov of tank engines. Russian military mechanics say the V2 was not only easy to maintain, but reliable in all weather conditions. The exception to this practical Soviet approach is the T-64 which was fitted with a copy of a German engine and was hindered by constant problems. Instead of adopting the proven V-2 engine, the T-14 Armata was given a new powerplant. While it's not clear why a different engine was selected, it may have been because of a lack of available components as a result of the Kharkiv factory being destroyed or the impact of Western sanctions on the availability of required computer chips. Whatever the reason, the Russian team selected a German style engine, which was designated the A-85 – 3. The engine chosen was originally designed for pumping stations rather than tanks. Engineers re-worked the A-85-3 for military use and it was conceived as the best product for the T-14. It is a small engine, complex, difficult to maintain and allegedly underpowered. It is believed that T-14 was designed around the engine and not the other way round which is unusual.

Tanks Costs

Russia's decision to build a totally new tank, the Armata, was an innovative move. But the cost of tank design and development is so high that many Western governments cannot afford the investment and consequently upgrades to existing types have been more appealing. Additionally, on the evidence of the current war in Ukraine, the future of tank warfare is by no means easy to predict. Hundreds of tanks and armoured vehicles have been destroyed in Ukraine by armed drones, operated and deployed by

one person. The financial equation is worrying for politicians who face pressure to build more tanks while reading reports of £200 drones that can chase and destroy Russian tanks costing millions and their crews.

Deployment in Ukraine

The war in Ukraine has seen most of Russia's armour hardware but not the T-14. Western observers claim this is due to the ongoing engine problems, while in Russia commanders said the tank *had* been deployed but was being held back for future operations. There was little evidence to support the claim. Moscow propaganda had suggested that the tank had been in the Donetsk region in support of T-72s, but despite the prevalence of social media imagery from the area, there were no pictures. Then in March 2024, the CEO of Russia's state-owned defence conglomerate, Rostec, Sergey Chemezov, finally confirmed that the tank has never been deployed in Ukraine for being too expensive and the T-90 being a more efficient option.

Moscow is unlikely to be using its new tank on the battlefield in Ukraine because the system is simply too costly with each tank estimated to cost between $6m and $7m. The embarrassment of losing a tank hailed by Putin as the best in the world would be too much for the Kremlin. For the time being the T-14 tank is effectively on hold , nothing has been heard of the venture since 2022 when Western intelligence claimed the Armata tank programme has been abandoned.

While complete abandonment is unlikely, the problem for Moscow has been the volume of microelectronics which Russian industry is reliant on imports for, and which modern arms are critically dependent on. These problems were evident across Europe during the Covid-19 epidemic when computer chips were not exported

from Taiwan in the numbers that had been before the global crisis. Car manufacturers in particular could not get chips to operate electric windows and radios resulting in delays in delivery. Russian corruption has also been blamed for the selection of the engine which on paper could not be more unsuited. In 2022 alone more than 50 defence industry managers and 200 public procurement officials were prosecuted.

Russia has also struggled to re-build its industry and tank production lines which relied heavily on Ukraine, and this may be a reason why the Armata did not make it into full production. Moscow needs tanks to resupply its war effort and has turned to funding assembly lines for cheap T-72B3s with a second factory refurbishing T-62s. The Russian army started the war with more than 3,600 operational tanks, of which around 1,000 had modern upgrades.

The T-14 was an expensive project that has thus far failed due to a lack of industrial power. Malcolm Williams, a former British Army tank commander believes the Armata will re-surface in a couple of years. Malcolm who served in Challenger tanks, said the Russian armoured units have a very 'singular and basic approach to tank warfare'. He said: " The Soviet model was to build thousands of tanks as cheaply as possible; they did not care about technology and smart tanks, they wanted mass, that was and always has been their philosophy. The T-14 was a move completely out of their comfort zone in the respect that it appears to be a tank for a thinking commander - a step change from the herd mentally of 'charge at the enemy'. But I am confident it will be back; Russia has little money to invest at the moment but this [the Armata] appears to be a project endorsed by Putin and that will be its saving grace."

T-14 ARMATA

Russia's new super-tank, the T-14 Armata, is an impressive hi-tech military platform which has advanced the design of main battle tanks with its unmanned turret, state-of-the-art sensors and computer systems as well as claims that its new armour can defend against any Western weapon currently in service. President Putin sees the tank as evidence that Russia is a world leader in military technology with the Armata being the first in a new line of armoured vehicles that will deliver fast, protective firepower to the Russian Army.

But while there is no question that the tank includes revolutionary design, it is unclear how capable the vehicle is. The Armata was designed in a five-year project, and while in the past Russian commanders have paid scant regard for either the protection, or the room given, to the crew the Armata is different. Among innovative characteristics, the crew of three is seated in an armoured 'fully protective' capsule in the front of the hull. Instead of the cramped conditions of previous Soviet era tanks where crews struggled for room and lacked situational awareness, the Armata crew sit in an open space with a bank of screens in front of them which provide live imagery of the battlefield. The crew's comfort also extends to the first crew toilet in a Russian tank.

Sensors on the hull provide the commandeer with a range of information in what the Kremlin claims is the most advanced tank in the world. Putin has stated that the Russian army will receive new tanks – traditionally the backbone of Moscow's ground forces – with the Armata spearheading the way, The T-14 Armata is the principle MBT variant, signifying Russia's first all-new tank design since the introduction of the Soviet T-80 some 40 years ago. In addition, a heavy Infantry Fighting Vehicle (IFV) called the T-15 has been developed. It is understood to have a 125mm gun fitted with a longer rear compartment which can carry as many as ten soldiers and will »

ARMATA T-14 MAIN BATTLE TANK SPECIFICATION

Model	ARMATA
Manufacturer	Uralvagonzavod
Country	Russia
Year	2014
Engine	12N360 Diesel Double Turbocharger
Fuel	Diesel
Protection	7039 aluminium alloy hulls, Rolled Homogeneous Steel turret
Top Speed	50mph surfaced road
Range	320 miles
Crew Capacity	Three
Length	35ft
Width	11ft
Height	11ft
Armament	2A82-1M 125mm smoothbore cannon
Weight	55 tonnes
Service Branch	Russia

refurbishments, the upgrades have been restricted by the design of the tanks' chassis. The T-14 is a clear indicator that Russia is moving, at least prior to the Ukraine war, away from the large scale tank formations of yesteryear and transitioning towards a smaller, more professional and less conscripted force. The overall design of the T-14, and its greater emphasis on crew protection and survivability suggests that commanders are planning a smaller force which will no longer be expendable as Soviet era tank crews were. The Armata's unmanned turret is the most revolutionary aspect of the T-14, and it is the first operational battle tank in the world to field this capability. Russia's past weakness has been to rely on ageing weapons and equipment, but it was Moscow's decision in the 1960s to adopt an autoloader system in the then T-64 tank that changed the manner in which Russian crews operated. The autoloader was seen as revolutionary, as it made the loader redundant and allowed tanks to incorporate a lower profile. Now the Kremlin's tank designers have produced an automatic turret – the most vulnerable and exposed area of the tank. It is unclear exactly how the turret functions and how the ammunition is loaded and what action is taken if a round jams in the breech. A major concern highlighted by Western tank commanders about the autoloader carousel was the fact that live rounds in the turret could result in a major catastrophic explosion if the turret is penetrated. It is presumed that ammunition is stored behind the crew's armoured capsule and is lifted to the turret on a hoist – but there is no indication as to how the crew rectify a minor stoppage in the hoist or auto-loader. In Soviet era tanks a failure in the autoloader resulted in the gunner slowly arming the breech by hand, which at least resulted in the tank remaining operational.

RIGHT: The controversial engine which was selected for the Armata. Russian MoD

transit troops to the forward edge of the battlefield (FEBA) then provide supporting fire for any infantry assault. A T-16 Armoured Recovery Vehicle (ARV) is also reported to be in production – but neither have been seen in public.

The move to generate new platforms come after decades in which the Russian administration has focused on updates of the T-72 and T-90 derivatives, with the emphasis on large numbers of armour which can defeat any enemy purely on scale of numbers. But while both the T-72 and T-90 tanks have seen various

RIGHT: According to the Russian defence ministry, the T-14 spent 12 months taking part in live firing trials. Russian MoD